Sugar, Cinnamon, and Love

VIRGINIA HORSTMANN

Sugar, Cinnamon, and Love

MORE THAN 70 ELEGANT CAKES, PIES, TARTS, AND COOKIES MADE EASY

Skyhorse Publishing

Table of Contents

FOREWORD

My name is Virginia—but everyone calls me Jeanny, ever since I can remember—and I absolutely love to eat cake. I am ecstatic if a kitchen knife slices through a smooth cheesecake, if candied pecans crunch between teeth, or if the scent of warm buttery streusel on a rhubarb cake tickles the nose with an aroma so great that it should be captured in pretty perfume bottles. Baking is my big passion, my time away from everyday life, my relaxing oasis. Instead of going to yoga, I sprinkle flour on my countertop, roll up my sleeves and knead the dough.

With each cake that I bake, I experience my childhood yet again, and with each bite, I remember all of the festive family gatherings and moments of happiness. The taste of Donauwelle cake reminds me of Uncle Herbert's wedding, the spice cake with extra thick icing brings back memories of each visit to Aunt Erna's house, and Frankfurter crown cake automatically makes me think of our old neighbor. Cake means to me, a piece of a perfect world; and therefore, there's not a weekend that goes by where a cake does not sit on the kitchen counter, waiting to be cut.

Two years ago, I realized that friends and family had started asking me for recipes more and more often, so on New Year's Day, I sat myself down at the computer at night and finally set about sharing my baking knowledge. The next morning, my food blog, *Zucker, Zimt und Liebe* (Sugar, Cinnamon, and Love), was born. Since then, dessert ingredients are not only measured and stirred in our kitchen, but the final products also photographed, with just as much passion. Because what could be better than sharing the sweetness of life with others?

As I signed the contract for this book, the fancy letters of my signature curving across the page, my heart was pounding, and I was fighting euphoria. A real baking spree lay ahead of me. Seventy-six recipes needed to be thought up, tried out, and the results beautifully presented. Countless bags of flour and sugar piled up in our kitchen, next to a good many cans of baking powder, and hundreds of vanilla beans and chocolate bars. The fridge was completely filled with butter, cream, and fruit from all over the world. I have braided dough into miniature works of art, tried many ideas that I ended up rejecting, tweaked and improved, styled and photographed. The people closest to me ended up tasting, judging, and getting excited about the goodies. Now all my friends and family have a little more fat on their hips, but also a bigger smile on their lips.

So that no one is excluded from this joy, the recipes are all fairly simple to make. You don't need a patisserie degree, nor professional equipment. The ingredients are varied so that there is something delicious here for everyone. In addition to little treats to snack on, there are also more extravagant options for special occasions, as well as desserts that lift your mood and make dreary days sweeter.

I hope you have a lot of fun while baking, and *bon appétit*!

ALL THE ♥ IN THE UNIVERSE,

Jeanny

SWEET LITTLE
Sins

You don't always need the huge multi-tiered cake, as sometimes
a sweet little morsel can be just as blissful. Here's a collection
of my favorite sins, in their miniature forms!

Favorite Madeleines

"Mama, did you bake shells?" As light and beautiful as if they were picked up from the beach, but much softer and sweeter, these French pastries are beauties that can be enjoyed by themselves, or also dipped in milk or coffee.

MAKES APPROX. 24 COOKIES
(depending on the size of the molds; I have a madeleine pan with small shells and can make approx. 40 madeleines out of the crust)

¾ cup (180 g) butter
4 eggs
⅔ cup + 3 tbsp (170 g) sugar
1 ⅓ cups (170 g) flour
2 tsp baking powder
1 pinch cinnamon
1 small pinch salt

♥

ADDITIONALLY:
Butter for the pan
Powdered sugar for dusting

1. Butter the molds of the madeleine pan well. Preheat the oven to 355°F (180°C).

2. Melt the butter in a small saucepan and allow to cool.

3. Put the eggs and sugar in a bowl, and beat about 5 minutes, until creamy.

4. Mix the flour, baking powder, cinnamon, and salt first, then sift, and mix with the egg-sugar mixture at a slow pace.

5. Add the melted butter and stir. Fill the molds with the dough, and bake in the oven for 8–10 minutes. The madeleines are done when the edges are slightly brown.

6. Carefully remove from the molds and dust generously with powdered sugar.

You can also cover the madeleines with icing, or whatever else tickles your fancy!

MY TIP

Raspberry-Mascarpone Mini Pies
WITH HEARTS

It's a shame that we can't put sweets in our children's lunchboxes. Really a pity, because otherwise our little charmer could bring these heart pies to the friend he sits next to every day, or even make the teacher melt by offering her one of these adorable delights . . .

MAKES 6 LITTLE PIES
(depending on the size of
the cookie cutter you've chosen,
of course)

♥

FOR THE DOUGH:
1 ⅔ cups (200 g) flour
1 pinch salt
½ tsp sugar
¾ cup + 1 ½ tbsp (105 g) very
    cold butter, cut into pieces
5 tbsp ice cold water

♥

FOR THE FILLING:
6 tbsp fresh raspberries
    (or frozen, but then almost
    completely thawed)
1 pinch cinnamon
2 tbsp sugar
6 tsp mascarpone

♥

ADDITIONALLY:
1 egg, whisked together with
    1 tbsp milk (or cream)

1. Mix flour, salt and sugar together to form a pie crust. Add the butter, and quickly knead the mixture until it is crumbly. Add water and quickly combine together, forming a dough. Don't knead the dough too much, or the quality of the crust will degrade. It should just barely hold together. Then press the dough slightly so that it flattens, wrap it in plastic wrap and place it in the refrigerator for at least ½ hour.

2. Meanwhile, prepare the filling: lightly crush the raspberries with a fork and mix with cinnamon and sugar.

3. Preheat the oven to 375°F (190°C). Line a baking sheet with parchment paper.

4. Take the dough out and let sit until it reaches room temperature. Then, quickly, roll it out thin, with as few strokes as possible, working from the center outwards. It should be approximately 1/10 in (3 mm) thick. Using a round cookie cutter, cut out 12 circles. Place half of them on parchment paper, and then put 1 teaspoon of mascarpone as well as 1 tablespoon of the raspberry mixture on each. Coat the edges with a little bit of beaten egg.

5. Cut out little hearts or stars from the remaining six circles. Then place these circles on top of the six which are covered with mascarpone and raspberries, and seal the edges firmly, by pressing down with a fork.

6. Brush the small pies with the remaining beaten egg and bake in the oven for about 20 minutes. The raspberries will bubble up beautifully, and I also don't find it so bad if some of the raspberry juice flows out of the heart. Sweet raspberry lava!

Mini Vanilla Poppy Seed Cakes

A dalmatian among cakes, this treat not only goes really well with my cute polka-dot dress, but also is great for picnics, and can be eaten on-the-go while enjoying a bike ride in the sun.

MAKES APPROX. 8 MUFFIN-SIZED LITTLE CAKES

1 ½ cups (190 g) flour

1 ⅓ cups + 1 tbsp (280 g) sugar

¼ teaspoon baking powder

1 pinch of salt

1 tbsp poppy seeds

½ cup (120 ml) milk

2 tbsp greek yogurt or crème fraîche

1 cup (240 ml) vegetable oil

3 eggs

Vanilla pulp, taken out of 1 pod

♥

FOR THE ICING:

¾ cup + 4 tsp (100 g) powdered sugar

1–2 tbsp milk

♥

ADDITIONALLY:

Butter and flour for the pan

1. Preheat the oven to 392°F (200°C). Butter and flour either a pan with molds for mini-cakes or a muffin tin.

2. Mix the flour, sugar, baking powder, salt and poppy seeds in a bowl, then set aside.

3. Mix milk, yogurt (or crème fraîche), oil, eggs and scraped out vanilla pulp in another bowl and add to the flour mixture. Stir everything together until a homogeneous mixture is obtained, but not longer. Too much mixing takes the fluffiness out of the cake.

4. Pour the batter into the prepared tins and bake in the oven for 20–25 minutes.

5. Mix powdered sugar and milk together to the desired consistency and pour icing over the cooled cakes.

LITTLE
Ricotta-Cherry Pop Tarts

Do you have a little Picasso in you? Do you like abstract art? Then get excited. Because here you can combine this passion with baking and spread sweet cherry juice icing masterfully and wildly across these little tarts. A true work of art—and a delicious reward immediately afterwards.

MAKES 6 SMALL TARTS
1 ⅓ cups (155 g) flour
2 tbsp (15 g) powdered sugar
1 pinch salt
⅓ cup (75 g) cold butter, cut
    into pieces
1 egg yolk
2 ¾ tbsp (40 ml) milk
4 tbsp ricotta, lightly stirred
4 tbsp cherry marmalade
1 egg, whisked together with
    1 tsp warm water

♥

FOR THE ICING:
¾ cup + 4 tsp (100 g) powdered
    sugar
1–2 tbsp cherry juice or milk

♥

ADDITIONALLY:
Flour for the countertop

1. Mix the flour, powdered sugar, and salt. Add the butter and rub with your hands until the mixture is crumbly. Add the egg yolk and milk and knead everything together into a smooth dough. Then flatten and wrap in plastic wrap. Store somewhere cold for at least ½ hour.

2. Preheat the oven to 374°F (190°C). Line a baking sheet with parchment paper.

3. Roll out the dough on a floured surface into a 16 x 9 in (40 x 23 cm) rectangle. Use a pastry wheel or a pizza cutter to cut 12 small rectangles. Lay them on a baking sheet.

4. Take half of the rectangles, spoon a little bit of ricotta onto them, and then a small amount of cherry marmalade. Brush the edges with beaten egg, and then place the remaining rectangles on top. Quickly seal each edge with a fork.

5. Bake the small tarts for 15 minutes in the oven and let cool.

6. Make a sweet glaze from powdered sugar and either cherry juice or milk, and distribute artfully on the tarts.

Apple Pie
WITH A TWIST

These apples aren't just lounging around in their pajamas today, but rather dressing up, by wrapping themselves up in delicious pastry. Plus, they're filled with nuts and cranberries, making them a real soul food. As soon as they come out of the oven, you should pour vanilla sauce over them and enjoy them, along with a good romantic movie on the couch.

MAKES 5–6 LITTLE APPLE PIES

♥

FOR THE DOUGH:
2 ⅓ cups (300 g) flour
1 tsp salt
1 cup (230 g) very cold butter,
   cut into pieces
¾ cup (180 ml) ice cold water

♥

FOR THE FILLING:
5–6 apples
1–2 tbsp lemon juice
3 tbsp Brazil nuts or walnuts
1 ½ tbsp granulated brown sugar
2 Amarettini cookies, crumbled
2 tbsp butter, cut into little pieces
2 tbsp cranberries, chopped

♥

ADDITIONALLY:
Flour for the countertop
1 egg, whisked together with
   1 tbsp milk
Vanilla sauce or vanilla ice cream
   for serving

1. For the dough, mix the flour and the salt. Then incorporate the butter quickly, until the dough is crumbly. Slowly add the ice cold water, and mix until a dough forms. Then place the dough onto the floured countertop and form into a ball using your hands. This should happen quickly so that the dough is not too warm.

2. Split the dough in half, wrap each piece in plastic wrap, and leave in the refrigerator for at least 2 hours. Afterwards, let the dough return to room temperature, so that it can be rolled out. In the meantime, peel the apples, and core using a corer. Rub with a little bit of lemon juice.

3. Prepare the filling by combining the chopped nuts, sugar, Amarettini, butter and cranberries.

4. Preheat the oven to 375°F (190°C). Roll out the dough thinly and distribute the apples across it evenly. Stuff the apples with the filling, then cut large circles around them and bring the edges of the dough up to the top of the apples. Seal the dough up well so it does not open during cooking. Seal up the top further with a little bit of beaten egg.

5. Brush the apple pies with the remaining egg. From the remaining pastry sheets cut out small leaves, brush them with egg as well, and decorate the mini pies with them. Place them in the oven on a baking sheet lined with parchment paper, and bake for about 25 minutes. Then, while they are still warm, cut them into slices, serve with vanilla sauce or ice cream, and enjoy.

Semlor – Swedish Buns
WITH MARZIPAN FILLING AND CREAM

These little pastries are perhaps the most delicious in the world. They are most often enjoyed in Sweden, and more than any other day, on Shrove Tuesday, which is the day before Lent begins. Today they are often found throughout all of Lent, up until Easter.

MAKES 10 SEMLOR

♥

FOR THE DOUGH:
1 cup (250 ml) low-fat milk
⅓ cup + 1 tbsp (100 g) butter
2 tsp dry yeast
1 pinch salt
3 tbsp + ½ tsp (40 g) sugar
1 egg
3 ⅔ cups (450 g) flour, plus
    possibly a little bit more

♥

FOR THE FILLING:
⅔ cup (150 ml) milk
5.3 oz (150 g) marzipan paste
1 ¼ cups (300 ml) cream

♥

ADDITIONALLY:
Powdered sugar, for garnishing

1. For the dough, bring the milk to a boil in a saucepan, then remove from heat quickly.

2. Put the butter in the milk and let it slowly melt. Then let cool until the mixture is lukewarm.

3. Pour the milk mixture into a bowl along with the remaining ingredients and mix everything together into a smooth dough. If it is too sticky, add a little flour, a tablespoon at a time.

4. Form the dough into about ten balls, and place them on a baking sheet lined with parchment paper. Cover with a paper towel and let rise in a draft-free, warm place for about 1 hour. After an hour, the size of the balls should have increased markedly.

5. Meanwhile, preheat the oven to 390°F (200°C). Bake the Semlor for about 15 minutes, and then let cool.

6. Use a sharp knife to cut open each Semlor and a spoon to hollow them out, so that the filling can be put in. Combine the hollowed out dough with the milk and marzipan and let soak until soft. Work these ingredients together until you have a smooth mass. Then put the filling inside of the Semlor.

7. Whip the cream until stiff and pipe on top of the filling. Put the top back on each Semlor, and garnish with powdered sugar.

Raspberry Friands

Small and sweet and juicy—and with a slightly tart and fresh surprise: scrumptious raspberries. That's how these perfect little cakes taste. The friands can also be baked in muffin cups, and made with either blueberries or strawberries.

MAKES APPROX.
12 MUFFINS OR 6–8
MINI-LOAVES
1 ⅓ cups (190 g) butter
½ cup (60 g) flour
1 ⅔ cups (200 g) powdered sugar
1 ¼ cups (120 g) very finely ground
   almonds
2 egg whites
Zest from 1 organic lemon
Raspberries (or other berries)
   as desired (also frozen)

♥

ADDITIONALLY:
Butter and flour
   for the pans

MY TIP

1. Preheat the oven to 355°F (180°C). Butter the pan and sprinkle lightly with flour.

2. Melt the butter in a small pot. Sift flour and powdered sugar into a bowl, and add the almonds (grind them well before adding so that they are fine enough).

3. Add in lightly whisked egg whites, melted butter, and lemon zest and mix well.

4. Pour batter into the tins until they are two-thirds full, cover with berries and bake 25–35 minutes in the oven.

Before eating the friands, if desired, garnish with chopped pistachios and powdered sugar, and serve with a glass of cold milk.

Galettes des Rois

Mon Dieu, this cake made out of puff pastry with almond and apricot stuffing can be found in almost any bakery in Paris. And they are so simple to make that I can easily conjure up memories of past trips to the city of love, in miniature form, from my very own oven.

MAKES 6 GALETTES

½ cup + 1 tbsp (125 g) room
    temperature butter
⅔ cup (125 g) sugar
1 ⅓ cups (130 g) ground almonds
1 tbsp cornstarch
1 pinch salt
2 eggs
2 rolls puff pastry from the
    refrigerated section (not frozen!)
6 tsp apricot marmalade

♥

ADDITIONALLY:
1 egg yolk, whisked together
    with 1 tbsp cream

1. Line two baking sheets with parchment paper.

2. Beat the butter until creamy. Mix the sugar, almonds, cornstarch, and salt and combine with the butter. Then gradually add the eggs. Place the almond paste in the fridge for about 2 hours.

3. Cut out six circles from the spread out puff pastry using either a glass or round cookie cutter, and place them on the baking sheets. Place 1 teaspoon of apricot jam on each circle, spread it out, and place a generous amount of almond paste on top. Brush the edges with a little bit of the egg-cream mixture.

4. With a little bit larger glass or cookie cutter, cut out six more circles. Use a knife to carve embellishments as desired: stars, zig-zags, whatever shape you prefer. Now place the decorated circles on top of the smaller ones and press the edges together slightly. Brush with the remaining egg-cream mixture, and keep in the refrigerator for ½ hour. Meanwhile, preheat the oven to 390°F (200°C).

5. Finally, bake the galettes for 15 minutes.

Little Orange Amerikaner Cookies

WITH CHAI ICING AND PISTACHIOS

Everyone in Germany knows these cookies from children's birthday parties and from the corner bakery: Amerikaner cookies, usually dipped in frosting and/or covered with a chocolate coating. Here is my attempt to breathe new life into this classic of German baking: a gentle kiss of chai tea, orange, and pistachio.

MAKES APPROX. 12 COOKIES
(depending on the size)

♥

FOR THE DOUGH:
⅓ cup + 1 ½ tbsp (100 g) room temperature butter
½ cup (100 g) sugar
2 tsp (8 g) vanilla sugar
1 pinch salt
2 eggs
2 cups (250 g) flour
(1 small packet) vanilla pudding mix
1 ½ tsp baking powder
3–4 tbsp milk
Zest from ½ of an organic orange

♥

FOR THE ICING:
1 tbsp butter
3 tbsp milk
1 tea bag Chai (or tea ball with Chai tea mix)
1 ⅔ cups (200 g) powdered sugar
Chopped pistachios for garnishing

1. Preheat the oven to 390°F (200°C). Line a baking sheet with parchment paper and set aside.

2. Beat the butter, sugar, vanilla sugar, and salt in a bowl until fluffy. Add in the eggs one at a time.

3. Mix the flour, pudding mix and baking powder, and then stir them into the batter. Add milk and orange zest, and mix well.

4. Use a piping bag to distribute the dough onto the baking sheet in several two tablespoon portions. Leave a good amount of distance between the blobs of dough, because the cookies spread out in all directions in the oven. (I therefore work with two batches, baking the first baking sheet with 6 cookies on it, and then baking another round. Better safe than sorry.)

5. Bake the Amerikaner cookies for 15–20 minutes in the oven, then briefly let cool, before placing them on a wire rack to let cool completely.

6. For the (super delicious) Chai icing, melt the butter in a small saucepan, add the milk and bring it to a very gentle simmer, then take the pot off the stove again. Place the tea bags in the liquid and leave them in for 3–4 minutes. Then squeeze the tea bags and remove them from the icing. Mix the powdered sugar in well and stir until a spreadable glaze forms. The Amerikaner cookies are frosted with this, and garnished with chopped pistachios.

Croissants

WITH GOAT CHEESE – CHOCOLATE FILLING

On Sunday morning, the smell of homemade croissants with goat cheese-chocolate filling drifts from your kitchen to the bedroom and tickles the nose of a little sleepyhead. Sound pleasant? It gets even better: you can teach your loved ones to make this recipe as well. It is extremely easy and rolling the croissants makes it especially fun for the little ones.

MAKES 16 CROISSANTS

♥

FOR THE DOUGH:
5 tbsp (60 g) sugar
1 pinch salt
5 tbsp milk
5 tbsp vegetable oil
4.4 oz (125 g) quark cheese (low-fat)
1 ⅔ cups (200 g) flour
2 tsp baking powder
1 egg yolk, whisked together with
    1 tbsp milk

♥

FOR THE FILLING:
1.8 oz (50 g) chocolate, coarsely
    chopped
1.8 oz (50 g) room temperature
    goat cream cheese
2 tbsp sugar

♥

ADDITIONALLY:
Flour for the countertop

1. For the filling, melt chocolate over a double boiler, and then let cool briefly. Combine with the goat cream cheese and the sugar in a bowl and mix with a hand mixer.

2. Preheat the oven to 355°F (180°C).

3. For the dough, mix sugar, salt, milk, oil and quark cheese in a bowl. Add flour and baking powder, and combine everything into a smooth dough. Then divide this into two portions.

4. Roll out each piece of dough into a circle on the floured countertop. Cut each circle first into quarters, and then cut each quarter in half (forming eighths). Put some of the chocolate cream on the wider ends of the dough pieces, and roll them tightly from the wide side in. Shape into crescents and set on a plate lined with parchment paper.

5. Brush the croissants with beaten egg and bake in the oven for 15–20 minutes.

Swedish Sugar Cookies

My family and I love Sweden. If we could, we would even build ourselves a home there, in the middle of the city, a traditional red Swedish house, made of wood. We were actually already in Bullerbü and hoped to meet Lasse, Bosse, Britta, Inga, Ole, Kerstin and Lisa (from the beloved German children's book series *Wir Kinder aus Bullerbü*). And of course we love Swedish delicacies—like these sugar cookies. A little bit of Bullerbü for home.

MAKES 16–18 SUGAR COOKIES
(depending on the size)
2 ¾ cups (340 g) flour, plus
    possibly a little bit more
⅔ cup + 3 tbsp (200 ml) milk
¼ cup (50 g) sugar
1 tbsp (10 g) baking powder
⅓ cup + 5 tsp (100 g) butter

♥

ADDITIONALLY:
1 egg, whisked
Coarse sugar, to be sprinkled
    on top

1. Preheat the oven to 390°F (200°C). Line a baking sheet with parchment paper.

2. Fill a bowl with flour, milk, sugar, and baking powder and mix together.

3. Melt the butter in a saucepan and add to the flour mixture. Knead everything together with your hands to form a dough. The dough should have a slightly sticky texture, but not too wet, so you can shape it into balls. If it is too wet, just add a little more flour and knead again.

4. Separate the dough into golf ball-sized pieces. Press holes in the center of the dough balls with your thumbs, and stretch each piece of dough so that you can shape it into a figure eight. Place each one on a baking sheet, brush with beaten egg and garnish with coarse sugar.

5. Bake the sugar cookies for about 15 minutes in the oven.

Pasteis de Nata

I admit, I've never been to Portugal. But these Portuguese mini tortes with cream filling make me really want to go there. At some point I'll persuade the rest of the family . . . The men will enjoy themselves in the ocean, while I'll be enjoying myself in a patisserie with one of these little tortes.

MAKES 12 PASTEIS DE NATA

1 roll puffed pastry from the refrigerated section (not frozen!)

1 ¼ cups (250 g) sugar

1 tbsp flour

2 cups + 2 tbsp (500 ml) whole milk

6 egg yolks

2 egg whites, stiffly beaten

♥

ADDITIONALLY:

Powdered sugar, to be sprinkled on top

1. Preheat the oven to 425°F (220°C). Get a muffin tin ready.

2. Don't unroll the puff pastry, but instead cut into twelve equal-sized pieces. Place each disc into a hollow of a muffin tin and using your hand, make small bowls out of the dough. When all twelve pasteis are ready, put the muffin tin briefly in the refrigerator.

3. Mix sugar and ⅓ cup + ¾ tbsp (100 ml) water in a saucepan and mix over medium heat to dissolve the sugar. Simmer for 10 minutes.

4. Combine the flour and milk and bring them to a boil in a different pot. Then, remove from heat and pour the sugar syrup in slowly. Mix well with a whisk, and let cool.

5. Add in the egg yolks and fold in the egg whites gently.

6. Pour the filling into the prepared tins and bake the pasteis de nata in the oven for about 15 minutes. The filling will naturally bubble and brown nicely.

7. Take these treats from the oven, let them cool slightly, and carefully remove them from the pan. Immediately sprinkle with powdered sugar and enjoy, preferably while they are still warm.

Donuts with Frosting
AND COLORFUL SPRINKLES

I really learned to love these sweet, sugary rings when I lived in Boston for a while. In the company where I completed an internship, there was a very tasty Tuesday tradition. Various departments got together, and over coffee and around 2,000 donuts, got to know each other better. Since I unfortunately cannot travel to Boston every Tuesday, I needed a recipe that brings back my memories.

MAKES APPROX. 10 DONUTS
(depending on the size)
4 tbsp dry yeast
1 cup (250 ml) lukewarm water
¼ cup (60 ml) lukewarm milk
3 tbsp fine sugar
½ cup (100 g) butter, melted
4 ½ cups + 1 tbsp (570 g) flour
3 eggs
1 pinch cinnamon

♥

FOR THE ICING:
¾ cup + 4 tsp (100 g) powdered
    sugar
1–2 tbsp milk
Food coloring
    (alternative: cinnamon sugar to
    toss the donuts in)

♥

ADDITIONALLY:
Flour for the countertop
Vegetable oil for baking
    (the pot should be filled with
    1 ½ – 2 in (4–5 cm) of oil)
Sprinkles or tiny chocolate hearts,
    for garnishing

1. Mix yeast, water, milk and 1 tablespoon sugar in a bowl and let rest for 5 minutes. By then, small bubbles should have formed on the surface.

2. Add in the butter, flour, eggs, remaining sugar, and cinnamon and on a floured countertop, knead into a smooth dough. Cover the dough and let it rise in a warm place for about 45 minutes, until the volume has doubled.

3. Knead the dough for another 5 minutes, until it feels smooth and elastic. Then roll it out until it is 1 cm thick, and cut donuts out of it. You can use a glass, and then a shot glass for the inner circle, if you do not have a donut cutter. Cover the dough rings, and let rest for ½ hour.

4. Heat up the oil in a saucepan. As soon as bubbles rise up from a submerged wooden spoon, fry the dough rings on both sides, one after another, until golden brown. Then fish them out and briefly let drain on paper towels.

5. If you want to, you can dip the donuts in cinnamon sugar now. Those who prefer icing can prepare one from powdered sugar, milk and food coloring. The icing should not be too liquidy, otherwise it drips off the donuts. Simply dip one side of the donut in icing, and then garnish to your heart's content with sprinkles or chocolate hearts.

Cinnamon-Buttermilk Ball Cupcakes

Some call it monkey bread. Maybe it's because it makes everyone start to act like little monkeys, jumping up and down, eagerly anticipating the delicious cinnamon rolls. Or because you can make another variety of them with bananas. I prefer to call them cinnamon-buttermilk ball cupcakes and am quite delighted with how easy they are to produce.

MAKES 12 CAKE BALLS

♥

FOR THE DOUGH:
2 cups (250 g) flour
3 tbsp sugar
1 tbsp baking powder
1 pinch salt
½ cup (120 ml) buttermilk
⅓ cup (80 ml) milk
⅓ cup (75 g) butter, melted

♥

FOR THE CRUST:
6 tbsp butter, melted
½ cup (100 g) granulated sugar
¾ cup (150 g) granulated brown
   sugar
1 tsp cinnamon

♥

FOR THE ICING:
⅔ cup + 3 tbsp (100 g) powdered
   sugar
1–2 tbsp milk

♥

ADDITIONALLY:
Butter for the pan

1. Preheat the oven to 345°F (175°C). Butter a muffin tin and set aside.

2. For the dough, sift flour, sugar, baking powder, and salt into a bowl. Add the buttermilk, milk and melted butter and quickly mix until a dough is formed.

3. For the crust, fill a sealable container with the half cup of granulated sugar.

4. Take small, teaspoon-sized portions of the dough, and form balls. Place them one by one into the sugar container, and shake well to coat the dough balls. Distribute six small sugared dough balls into each cup of the muffin pan.

5. Mix the butter with the granulated brown sugar and cinnamon. Spread this mixture on top of the cupcakes, and put the muffin tin in the oven for about 20 minutes.

6. After baking and cooling, mix the powdered sugar and milk together, take the cupcakes out of the muffin tin and drizzle with the glaze.

Apple-Mango Crumble

IN GLASSES

Nothing is more of a soul food to me than streusel on apples, straight from the oven. Every time my taste buds call for more than a plain apple, buttery crumble is placed on top. I have always been for filling perfume bottles with the smell of streusel. It would be my favorite fragrance, definitely!

MAKES 6 GLASSES
2 small apples
A splash of lemon juice
1 mango
1 tbsp cornstarch
2 tbsp butter

♥

FOR THE STREUSEL:
¾ cup + 2 ½ tsp (100 g) flour
¼ cup (50 g) sugar
1 tsp (4 g) vanilla sugar
1 pinch salt
1 pinch cinnamon
¼ cup (60 g) room temperature
   butter

1. Preheat the oven to 345°F (175°C). Peel, core and dice the apples. Immediately drizzle with lemon juice. Peel the mango as well, get rid of its core, cut it into cubes and mix with the apples in a bowl.

2. Mix the fruit with cornstarch and distribute into six oven-safe glasses. Put little pieces of butter on top.

3. For the streusel, mix flour, sugar, vanilla sugar, salt and cinnamon together. Add small pieces of butter, and knead into the streusel with your hands. Then sprinkle the streusel over the apples.

4. Bake for 25–30 minutes in the oven.

The Apple-Mango Crumble tastes especially delicious with creamy vanilla sauce.

MY TIP

Sweet Potato Muffins

WITH CINNAMON SUGAR CRUST

My husband loves, more than anything, his fried chicken cooked in the oven, alongside a variety of grilled vegetables. I think that one of these vegetables can also go very well in a muffin tin, covered with cinnamon and sugar, and turned into delicious delicacies: gorgeous orange sweet potatoes, transformed into something even more wonderful inside of a pastry.

MAKES 10 MUFFINS

2 ½ cups (300 g) flour

1 ½ tsp baking powder

1 pinch salt

¼ tsp baking soda

⅓ cup (80 ml) buttermilk

⅓ cup (80 ml) whole milk

1 large sweet potato, cooked
   and mashed into a puree

½ cup (115 g) room temperature
   butter

½ cup + 3 tbsp (135 g) granulated
   brown sugar

2 eggs

♥

FOR THE CRUST:

⅓ cup (70 g) sugar

2 tsp cinnamon

¼ cup (55 g) butter

♥

ADDITIONALLY:

Butter and flour for the pan
   (alternatively, paper muffin liners)

1. Preheat the oven to 345°F (175°C). Butter a muffin tin and lightly dust with flour. Alternatively, place ten paper cupcake liners in the trays.

2. Thoroughly mix flour, baking powder, salt and baking soda together in a bowl.

3. Mix buttermilk, milk and mashed sweet potato in another bowl.

4. Beat butter and granulated brown sugar together until fluffy. Gradually add the eggs. Taking turns, add the flour and milk mixtures alternatively, while continuing to mix. Fill ten muffin cups halfway with batter and bake in the oven for 20–25 minutes.

5. For the crust, mix sugar and cinnamon. Melt the butter. Once the muffins are finished baking, brush them quickly with butter and roll in cinnamon sugar.

FOR THE
Cake Plate

There are so many reasons to bake a delicious cake. A thousand reasons, and
at least as many different types of cakes. It would be hard for me to name a
favorite cake. I like to try out new recipes, from fruit cake to pound cake, to little
treats on a baking sheet. My oven has quite a few hours of heating work under
its belt, and is not tired. Just like me and my appetite . . .

Crème Fraîche Cake

WITH RASPBERRIES

The creamy crème fraîche in the batter and the crunchy sugar crust on top create a heavenly fruity liaison with the raspberries. One of my favorite summer cakes, fresh and light! Fortunately, the raspberry bushes in our garden are thriving.

FOR 1 LOAF PAN
(APPROX. 10 IN/25 CM)

♥

FOR THE DOUGH:
1 ⅓ cups + 1 tbsp (175 g) flour
1 tsp baking powder
1 pinch salt
1 pinch baking soda
½ cup (115 g) room temperature
  butter
¾ cup (150 g) sugar
2 eggs
¾ cup + 1 tbsp (200 g) crème
  fraîche
7 oz (200 g) raspberries (frozen
  fruit also works well here, but
  then do not thaw before baking)
2 tbsp granulated brown sugar

♥

FOR THE ICING:
¾ cup + 1 tbsp (100 g) powdered
  sugar
1–2 tbsp milk

♥

ADDITIONALLY:
Butter and flour for the pan
A few raspberries for garnishing

1. Preheat the oven to 345°F (175°C). Butter the loaf pan and lightly dust it with flour.

2. For the dough, sift the flour, baking powder, salt, and baking soda in a bowl, and set aside.

3. In another bowl, beat butter and sugar with a hand mixer until creamy. Gradually add the eggs.

4. Alternate adding the flour mixture and the crème fraîche to the egg mixture while continuing to stir.

5. Carefully fold in the raspberries (if you use frozen raspberries, you do not have to be quite as careful) and pour the batter into the prepared pan. Sprinkle with granulated brown sugar.

6. Put the pan in the oven and bake the cake for 60–70 minutes. Place a toothpick into the center of the cake to test whether or not it is ready (i.e., if nothing clings to it after insertion), because remember, every oven cooks differently. Then let cool.

7. Stir the powdered sugar and milk together into a glaze and decorate the cake with it.

8. Place a few especially beautiful raspberries on top.

Strawberry Coconut
CAKE

He wants coconut cake, she'd rather have strawberry? For such problems taking place in the kitchen on Saturday afternoons, the world of baking keeps a relationship-friendly compromise solution ready: the easy to make, quick, deliciously fresh strawberry and coconut cake. Everything is going to be OK!

FOR 1 SPRINGFORM PAN
(8 IN / 20 CM)

1 ⅔ cups flour (220 g, plus 2 tbsp
    extra)
1 ½ tsp baking powder
1 pinch salt
⅔ cup (50 g) coconut flakes
¾ cup + 1 tbsp (190 g) room
    temperature butter
¾ cup + 1 tbsp (160 g) sugar
3 eggs
4 tbsp coconut milk (alternatively,
    whole milk)
Approx. 10 strawberries, washed
    and quartered

♥

ADDITIONALLY:
Butter for the pan
1 ⅔ cups (400 ml) cream
2 tbsp powdered sugar

1. Preheat the oven to 355°F (180°C). Butter and lightly flour the springform pan and line the bottom with parchment paper.

2. Sift the flour, baking powder and salt into a bowl. Add the coconut flakes to the mixture and set aside.

3. In another bowl, beat the butter and sugar with an electric mixer until creamy. Gradually add the eggs.

4. Now, alternate adding in the flour mixture and the coconut milk (or whole milk) to the butter mixture.

5. Pour the batter into the prepared pan. Toss the strawberry quarters briefly into 2 tablespoons flour, and then place on the cake, forming a circle.

6. Place the pan in the oven for 20 minutes. Then reduce the temperature to 320°F (160°C) and bake the cake for another 45–50 minutes. Use the toothpick test to see whether or not the cake has cooked long enough. Finally, take it out of the oven and let cool.

7. Now beat the whipping cream with an electric mixer until stiff and gradually add powdered sugar. Serve with the cake.

Mallorcan Almond Cake

IN A BUNDT PAN

Here, we substitute flour with finely ground almonds and make this bundt cake a fluffy, light afternoon coffee cake, reminiscent of holidays on the sunny island.

FOR 1 SMALL BUNDT PAN
OR 1 SPRINGFORM
(9 IN / 23 CM)
1 ⅓ cups (200 g) almonds,
    blanched
5 eggs, separated
1 cup (200 g) sugar
Zest from 1 organic lemon

♥

ADDITIONALLY:
Butter and flour for the pan
Powdered sugar and slivered
    almonds, for garnishing

1. Preheat the oven to 340°F (170°C).

2. Butter the pan very well and lightly flour (tap out surplus flour, or the cake will not look the way it should after baking and cooling, and that would be a shame).

3. Grind the almonds very finely in a food processor. If you do not have one, you can use a package of ground almonds without grinding them again.

4. Beat the egg yolks and sugar in a bowl until creamy and add lemon zest. Combine this with the ground almonds.

5. Beat egg whites with a sanitized mixer until stiff. Add some of the egg whites to the almond mixture and stir well so that the dough can accept their addition. Then gently fold in the remaining egg whites with a spatula.

6. Then fill the prepared pan with the dough, stretching it flat over the top, to ensure that it is evenly distributed. Bake in the oven for approximately 40 minutes, until the toothpick comes out clean.

7. Allow the cake to cool completely and then remove it from the pan. Garnish with powdered sugar and sliced almonds.

MY TIP

If you want to, you can throw a handful of finely chopped chocolate under the dough before you fill the cups.

Hummingbird

CAKE

Many myths surround this cake, which try to explain the origin of its existence. But it shouldn't matter to us where it comes from: When pineapple, banana and coconut meet and decide to get together in a delicious dough, you get a succulent cake that tastes a bit like Jamaica.

FOR 1 SQUARE BAKING PAN
(8 X 8 IN / 20 X 20 CM)

♥

FOR THE DOUGH:
1 ½ cups (190 g) flour
1 tsp baking powder
1 pinch salt
½ tsp baking soda
1 tsp cinnamon
1 cup (200 g) granulated
   brown sugar
15.9 oz (450 g) pineapple in
   chunks (1 can)
1 cup (70 g) coconut flakes
2 bananas, peeled and cut into pieces
2 eggs
1 cup + 1 tbsp (120 ml) vegetable oil

♥

FOR THE FROSTING:
¼ cup (50 g) cream cheese (full fat)
5 tsp (25 g) room temperature butter
2 cups (250 g) powdered sugar
1–2 tbsp milk

♥

ADDITIONALLY:
Butter for the pan
1 handful chopped walnuts

1. Preheat the oven to 355°F (180°C). Line the baking pan with parchment paper and lightly butter the sides.

2. For the dough, place flour, baking powder, salt, baking soda, cinnamon and sugar in a bowl and mix.

3. Drain the pineapple pieces, taking care to collect ⅓ cup (80 ml) of the juice. Add both of these, along with coconut flakes, bananas, eggs, and oil to the flour mixture and mix well with a hand mixer or food processor.

4. Then fill the pan with the batter and bake in the oven for approximately 45 minutes. Briefly let cool, and then place on a cooling rack.

5. For the frosting, mix cream cheese and butter until creamy. Add in powdered sugar, and depending on the consistency desired, also mix in a little milk. Spread the frosting onto the cake and garnish with chopped walnuts. Cut into pieces before serving.

Battenberg Cake

A true British classic, this cake, coated with marzipan, looks a bit like a chess board when it's cut. Your best bet is to just let your tea-time guests guess how this colorful cake could have possibly been made.

FOR 2 LOAF PANS
(3 X 8 IN / 8 X 20 CM)
1 ⅓ cups (175 g) flour
½ tsp baking powder
1 pinch salt
¾ cup (175 g) room temperature
    butter
¾ cup + 2 tbsp (175 g) sugar
3 eggs, whisked
Red food coloring
4 tbsp apricot marmalade,
    mixed well
1 marzipan cover (roll)

♥

ADDITIONALLY:
Butter and flour for the pan

1. Preheat the oven to 355°F (180°C). Butter the pans and sprinkle with flour.

2. Sift the flour, baking powder, and salt into a bowl, and set aside.

3. Beat the butter and sugar until creamy with an electric mixer. Add the eggs, then add the flour mixture gradually and mix well.

4. Divide the dough into two pieces of the same size. Color one portion carefully with a little bit of food coloring. Then place one piece of dough in each pan, and bake in the oven for about ½ hour (test with a toothpick!).

5. Allow to cool, then cut both cakes in half lengthwise, so that you have two equal-sized cake strips of the same color. (If the cake has risen too much, then cut the top off as necessary, so that all of the sides are straight.)

6. With the help of apricot jam, bind a red strip of cake and a yellow strip of cake together. Then spread the top of both of these strips with jam. Place the two remaining pieces of cake on top, with the order of colors reversed.

7. Now spread the entire cake with the remaining apricot jam. Roll out the marzipan and wrap it around the cake. Cut off the excess edges.

Cinnamon Squares

These handy cinnamon squares fit in any handbag. In theory. Because in practice they won't survive the way from the baking pan to the serving plate.

FOR 1 BAKING PAN
(8 X 12 IN / 20 X 30 CM)
1 cup (230 g) room temperature
    butter
1 cup (200 g) granulated brown
    sugar
1 cup + 1 tbsp (110 g) white sugar
½ tsp baking soda
1 large pinch cinnamon
1 pinch salt
2 eggs
1 ⅓ cups (275 g) flour
4–6 tbsp cinnamon sugar

♥

ADDITIONALLY:
Butter and flour for the baking pan

1. Preheat the oven to 345°F (175°C). Butter the baking pan and sprinkle lightly with flour.

2. Cream the butter and both sugars together in a bowl.

3. Add baking soda, cinnamon and salt. Then add the eggs, and finally, the flour. Mix until thoroughly combined.

4. Spread the dough out in the prepared pan, and then bake in the oven for about ½ hour. Immediately after that, sprinkle with cinnamon sugar.

5. After cooling, cut the cinnamon squares into pieces and serve. Don't forget: Before serving others, be sure to try them out yourself, and enjoy.

Cherry Banana

CHEESECAKE

I don't know what we preferred more as kids: watching the spectacle of both juices as they were poured, flowing into a glass and becoming so beautifully mixed, or the delicious taste. I have created a cherry-banana cheesecake from this memory that tastes fruity-fresh and has, up until now, impressed all houseguests who also love cheesecake.

FOR 1 SPRINGFORM
(8 IN / 20 CM DIAMETER)

♥

FOR THE CRUST:
7 tbsp (100 g) butter, melted
7 oz (200 g) whole grain
    shortbread cookies,
    finely crumbled
2 tbsp sugar

♥

FOR THE FILLING:
2 cups (450 g) room temperature
    cream cheese
¾ cup (150 g) sugar
1 ½ tbsp flour
2 eggs
7 tbsp (100 g) sour cream
1 large, very ripe banana,
    peeled and finely chopped

♥

FOR THE CHERRY TOPPING:
1 large jar (24 oz / 680 g)
    cherries (regular or morello),
    dried very well
½ cup (100 g) sugar
4 tbsp cherry juice
1 ½ tbsp cornstarch

1. Line the bottom of the springform pan with parchment paper. Preheat the oven to 345°F (175°C).

2. Beat the butter with the shortbread cookies and sugar, mix well. Spread out on the bottom of the pan. Press down firmly and refrigerate.

3. Briefly mix the cream cheese with a hand mixer until fluffy. Mix the sugar and flour, add to the cream cheese and mix everything until smooth. Add the eggs one by one, then stir in the sour cream, and lastly the banana.

4. Pour the cream cheese mixture into the prepared pan and spread out flat. Wrap the outside of the springform pan with plentiful aluminum foil. Then put the pan into a deep, large baking dish and fill it with hot water, so that the springform is halfway covered. Then carefully place it in the oven. (The hot water bath helps with uniform baking and prevents cracks from occurring in the cheesecake.)

5. Bake the cake for about 45 minutes. It will appear a little soft in the middle, but firms up as it cools. Leave the baking dish in the switched off oven for 1 hour. Then remove, set in the refrigerator, and let cool overnight.

6. Before serving, prepare the cherry sauce. Mix all of the ingredients for this in a pot, and bring to a boil. After 2 minutes, the sauce should be slightly thickened, and taken off the stove. After it has been cooled for a short time, it can be poured over the cake.

SWEDISH
Almond Cake

This is the simplest cake that I know. Even so, it is extremely soft, and will remain like that for a few days. You can, of course, serve this almond cake with blueberries and whipped cream, but eaten just as it is, fresh from the oven, it is also a real hit.

FOR 1 SPRINGFORM
OR OVEN-SAFE PAN
(8 OR 9 ½ IN / 20 OR 24 CM
DIAMETER)
½ cup (115 g) butter
1 cup (200 g) sugar
Zest from 1 organic lemon
2 eggs
1 pinch salt
Vanilla beans, taken out of
   1 pod
1 cup (120 g) flour
1 handful slivered almonds
2 tbsp sugar for sprinkling

♥

ADDITIONALLY:
Butter for the pan

1. Preheat the oven to 345°F (175°C). Lightly butter a springform or oven-safe pan.

2. Melt the butter in a pot and set aside.

3. Place sugar and lemon zest in a bowl. Combine by rubbing together with a flat spoon or mortar. What a scent!

4. Add the eggs, and mix everything using a whisk. Add the salt and vanilla pulp. Then stir in the flour.

5. Add in the melted butter, work into a smooth batter and fill the prepared pan with this.

6. Distribute the almonds on top of the dough, and then sprinkle sugar on top.

7. Bake the cake for 25–30 minutes, depending on the size of the pan and the properties of the oven. They have minds of their own from time to time, these appliances.

Berry Marble Cake

I used to prefer eating mostly just the chocolate part of the marble cake. Nowadays, I replace cocoa with fresh berries, and still look forward to every time I cut into the cake and see the interplay of colors, those lovely violet swirls.

FOR 1 BUNDT PAN
(HOLDS APPROX. 2 LITER)
3 cups (375 g) flour
4 ¼ tsp (15 g) baking powder
1 cup + 1 tbsp (250 g) room
    temperature butter
1 ¼ cups (250 g) sugar
1 pinch salt
4 eggs
1 cup (125 ml) milk
5.3 oz (150 g) blueberries

♥

FOR THE ICING:
1 ¼ cups (100 g) powdered sugar
1–2 tbsp raspberry juice
    (alternatively: milk and a little bit
    of food coloring)

♥

ADDITIONALLY:
Butter and flour for the pan
A few blueberries for garnishing

1. Preheat the oven to 345°F (175°C). Butter and lightly flour the bundt pan. Tap the excess flour out.

2. Sift together the flour and baking powder. Then set aside in a bowl.

3. Beat butter, sugar, and salt in a separate bowl, and use a hand mixer to beat until fluffy. Gradually add the eggs.

4. Alternate adding the flour mixture and the milk, each only a little at a time, all the while continuing to stir. Then remove one-third of the batter.

5. Finely puree the blueberries with an immersion blender, and mix that puree thoroughly with the third of the dough that was removed.

6. The light-colored dough and the blueberry dough now are both placed in the pan in turns and are mixed slightly, using a fork.

7. Bake the marble cake for about 1 hour in the oven, allow to cool, and remove from the pan.

8. Mix a glaze out of powdered sugar and raspberry juice, or powdered sugar, milk, and a little bit of food coloring, and pour over the cooled cake. Garnish with blueberries.

All-time Favorite Birthday Cake

WITH RASPBERRY FILLING AND CREAM

Happy Birthday! Or not, because this layer cake is also, on non-birthdays, a beautiful Sunday-in-the-garden-sitting-under-cherry-trees variety of cake. I didn't place my favorite flowers in a vase next to the cake in this case, but rather directly on top of it.

FOR 2 SPRINGFORM PANS
(8 IN / 20 CM DIAMETER)

♥

FOR THE DOUGH:
1 cup (200 g) sugar
¾ cup + 2 tbsp (200 g) room
    temperature butter
4 eggs, lightly whisked
1 ⅔ cups (200 g) flour
2 tsp baking powder
2 tbsp milk

♥

FOR THE FILLING AND
THE FROSTING:
3 tbsp + 1 tsp (25 g) room
    temperature butter
3 ½ tbsp (50 g) cream cheese
    (full fat)
2 cups (250 g) powdered sugar
1 cup (250 ml) cream
Approx. 5 tbsp raspberry
    marmalade (or more, entirely up
    to you)

♥

ADDITIONALLY:
Butter and flour for the pans

1. Preheat the oven to 375°F (190°C). Butter the springform pan and sprinkle with flour.

2. Mix all of the ingredients for the batter well with an electric mixer or food processor, until a homogeneous, creamy mass forms. Divide the batter evenly between both springform pans and bake for about 20 minutes. Remove from oven and let cool.

3. For the filling, beat the butter, cream cheese and powdered sugar until creamy. Do not despair, this may take several minutes. Everything will turn out alright!

4. Beat the cream to stiff peaks, and swiftly fold in 3 tablespoons of the cream cheese mixture. Set the remaining cream cheese mixture aside, as this is the frosting.

5. If desired, strain the raspberry jam through a colander, to remove the seeds.

6. Place one of the two layers of cake upside down (i.e., with the flat underside facing up) onto a cake plate, and spread with raspberry jam. Then top with cream, and finally put the second layer of cake on top. This time, the flat side faces down.

7. Spread the rest of the cream cheese frosting over the cake. It's no problem if some of it runs down the side. I think that even adds to the charm of these homemade treats. We're not a patisserie, eh?

Plum Jam Almond Cake

WITH CARDAMOM

Plum jam on bread is always good. I've made jam myself for years, and the pitting of plums, while sitting at my kitchen island and listening to music, is already a late summer ritual for me. Why then do we not even try to use this delicious fruit as an ingredient in cakes? I have tested it and am thrilled. Sweet cake, laced with slightly spicy and sour plum jam, with slivered almonds on top, is a combination that works beautifully.

FOR 1 RECTANGULAR BAKING TIN OR 1 ROUND SPRINGFORM PAN (9 ½ IN / 24 CM DIAMETER)

1 ¾ cups + 1 tbsp (225 g) flour
1 tsp baking powder
1 pinch salt
1 pinch ground cardamom
½ cup + ½ tbsp (120 g) room
    temperature butter
¾ cup (150 g) sugar
2 eggs
½ cup + 1 tbsp (125 ml) milk
4 tbsp plum jam
4 tbsp slivered almonds

♥

ADDITIONALLY:
Butter for the pan
Powdered sugar, for garnishing

1. Preheat the oven to 340°F (170°C). Butter the pan well, and line with parchment paper.

2. Mix flour, baking powder, salt, and cardamom and sift into a bowl.

3. Cream butter and sugar in another bowl with the hand mixer. Gradually add eggs.

4. Then alternately add milk and the flour mixture, and mix everything into a homogeneous, creamy dough.

5. Pour the batter into the pan, and with a small spoon, place several dots of plum jam on top. With a wooden skewer or fork, embellish with small swirls and sprinkle with slivered almonds.

6. Bake the cake for 30–35 minutes in the oven. Let cool, and dust with powdered sugar.

Chai Tea
CAKE

It's tea time! And what goes well with that is a juicy chai tea cake that is wonderfully velvety. Anyone who does not like chai can use any other tea to flavor the milk in this recipe, creating a different, unique tea experience.

FOR 1 LOAF PAN
(APPROX. 10 IN / 25 CM)
¼ cup (60 ml) milk
3 tea bags chai (alternatively,
   0.2 oz / 6 g loose tea in a
   tea strainer)
1 cup + 2 tbsp (150 g) flour
¾ cup (100 g) ground almonds
2 tsp baking powder
1 pinch salt
1 cup (200 g) sugar
Zest and juice from 1 organic
   lemon
¼ cup (60 ml) vegetable oil
5.3 oz (150 g) plain yogurt
   (3.5% fat)
2 eggs, lightly whisked
1 handful slivered almonds

♥

ADDITIONALLY:
Butter and flour for the pan

1. Preheat the oven to 345°F (175°C). Butter the loaf pan and sprinkle with flour.

2. Heat the milk in a saucepan and add the tea bags. Then remove from heat and let stand for about 10 minutes.

3. Mix flour, ground almonds, baking powder, salt, sugar and lemon zest in a bowl.

4. In another bowl, combine oil, yogurt, lemon juice, and the tea milk. Add the flour mixture and add the eggs. Stir until a homogeneous batter forms.

5. Fill the prepared pan with dough, garnish with the slivered almonds, and bake in the oven for about 45 minutes. Test with a toothpick to see if the cake is finished baking.

6. Allow to cool and then remove from pan.

Apple-Carrot Cake

WITH WALNUTS AND HONEY GLAZE

Carrot cakes are so nice and juicy and fresh that even vitamin haters will not say no here. By the way, I was still able to smuggle some apple into this recipe, because . . . How does you say it again? An apple a day . . .

FOR 1 SPRINGFORM PAN
(8 IN / 20 CM DIAMETER)

1 handful walnuts

4 ⅓ cups (250 g) sugar

12.3 oz (350 g) grated carrots

7 oz (200 g) grated organic apple
   with skin

1 cup (100 g) ground almonds

1 cup + 1 tbsp (150 g) flour

1 ⅓ cups + 1 tbsp (150 g)
   bread crumbs

2 ½ tsp baking powder

1 pinch salt

½ tsp cinnamon

Zest from ½ organic orange

1 pinch powdered ginger, to taste

3 large eggs

⅔ cup (150 ml) vegetable oil

♥

FOR THE ICING:

⅔ cup + 3 tbsp (100 g) powdered
   sugar

2 tbsp honey

1 ½ tbsp milk

♥

ADDITIONALLY:

Butter and flour for the pan

1. Preheat oven to 345°F (175°C). Line the pan with parchment paper, butter the edges, and sprinkle with flour.

2. Spread the walnuts out on a baking sheet and roast in the oven for about 5 minutes. In a nonstick skillet, let ½ cup (100 g) of sugar slowly caramelize over medium heat. I always stand by and continue stirring, rather than walking away from the stove. Mix well, and as soon as the sugar has turned into liquid caramel, quickly add the walnuts into the pan and mix everything together. Then place onto parchment paper, let cool, and chop coarsely.

3. Mix carrots, apple, almonds and chopped walnuts in a bowl and set aside. In another bowl, mix flour, bread crumbs, baking powder, salt, cinnamon, orange zest, and if you choose to, a little bit of ginger.

4. Beat the eggs and the rest of the sugar until creamy, adding in the oil a little at a time. Then stir in the flour mixture with a whisk, and finally, add the apple and carrot mixture. The batter will be very viscous. But this is also a dense autumn pound cake, no delicate cupcake.

5. Pour the mixture into the pan and bake in the oven for about 45 minutes. When the cake comes out of the oven, before it is too hard and dry, do the toothpick test—in the middle, it can be quite soft. Finally, let the cake cool.

6. For the delicious honey glaze, mix all of the ingredients well. If it gets too runny, add more powdered sugar. If it is too thick, add milk, very carefully, one teaspoon at a time. Pour the glaze over the cake, and it's ready to eat.

Rhubarb Cake

WITH ALMONDS

Years ago, my husband asked whether rhubarb was a woman's vegetable. Might be. I am a woman and I love rhubarb. And I get excited every time I'm eating this cake, and a sweet, yet sour piece of pink stem dances on my tongue.

FOR 1 SPRINGFORM PAN
(8 IN / 20 CM DIAMETER)

¾ cup + 2 ½ tsp (100 g) flour

1 pinch salt

1 tsp baking powder

1 ¼ cups (150 g) room temperature butter

¾ cup (150 g) sugar

2 eggs

2 cups + 5 tsp (200 g) ground almonds

14 oz (400 g) rhubarb without green, peeled and cut into large pieces

2 tbsp slivered almonds

1 tbsp granulated brown sugar

♥

ADDITIONALLY:
Butter for the pan   MY TIP

1. Preheat the oven to 355°F (180°C). Line the springform pan with parchment paper and butter the edges.

2. Mix flour, salt, and baking powder in a bowl, then set aside.

3. Mix butter and sugar with a hand mixer until light and creamy. Add the eggs in gradually, and then add the ground almonds and flour. Mix everything well.

4. Pour the batter into the prepared pan, and place the rhubarb in a fan shape on top. Then garnish with slivered almonds and sprinkle with granulated brown sugar.

5. Bake 60–70 minutes in the oven. If the cake is too brown, you can cover the pan with aluminum foil for the last 15 minutes.

6. Finally, let the cake cool, and remove it from the pan.

If desired, you can also sprinkle the rhubarb cake with powdered sugar or serve with a delicious scoop of vanilla ice cream.

Banana-Cinnamon Rolls

WITH WALNUTS AND MAPLE SYRUP GLAZE

I will admit that these banana-cinnamon rolls take time and are not just magically conjured up when acute cases of cinnamon roll munchies arise, but every minute of the wait is worth it.

MAKES 10–12 ROLLS

⅔ cup (160 ml) milk

½ cup + 1 tsp (120 g) butter

2 tbsp vegetable oil

2 ¼ tsp dry yeast

¼ cup (50 g) sugar

1 pinch salt

1 egg yolk

3 ⅔ cups (450 g) flour

3 very ripe bananas, peeled and
    mashed well

1 tbsp cornstarch

¼ tsp baking powder

7 tbsp granulated brown sugar

2 tsp cinnamon

1 handful walnuts, coarsely chopped

♥

FOR THE ICING:

1 ¾ oz (50 g) cream cheese
    (full fat)

2 tbsp (25 g) room temperature
    butter

1 cup (200 g) powdered sugar

1 tbsp maple syrup

♥

ADDITIONALLY:

Flour for the countertop

Butter for the pan

1. Heat the milk with ⅓ cup (40 g) butter in a saucepan, until the butter has melted. Remove the pan from the heat, add oil and let it cool completely. Then add yeast, stir briefly and let stand for 5 minutes. Then pour the liquid into a bowl. Add the sugar, salt, egg yolk, 2 cups (240 g) of flour, and mashed banana, and mix everything well.

2. Mix another 1 ⅓ cups (180 g) flour with the cornstarch and then combine with the dough. Cover with a small towel and let rise in a warm, draft-free place for about 1 ½ hours.

3. Mix the remaining flour with baking powder and add to the dough. Knead again, thoroughly. If the dough is too wet and not possible to roll out (try to test this with your fingers), gradually add flour by the tablespoon until the dough is able to be rolled out.

4. On the floured surface, roll out into a rectangle. Melt the remaining butter and brush the dough with it. With sugar, cinnamon (and love, of course) as well as the chopped walnuts, cover evenly and roll up tightly from the narrower side. With a sharp knife, cut approximately ¾-inch (2 cm) wide cinnamon rolls and place into a buttered baking dish. The cinnamon rolls must not be placed next to each other, as they expand while baking and will become closer and closer together.

5. Set the cinnamon rolls aside again, for 40 minutes. In the meantime, preheat the oven to 345°F (175°C). Then bake in the oven for 25 minutes (or until well browned).

6. For the icing, mix all of the ingredients well, and pour over the still warm cinnamon rolls.

Cheesecake

WITH GOAT CREAM CHEESE, FIGS, AND HONEY

I love cheesecake! When I was younger, I always craved my mom's, made from quark and custard filling. I also particularly like the rich New York variety, or as shown here, a more exotic version, with mild goat cheese, figs, and honey. Tastes like a warm day on a Mediterranean vacation under olive trees.

FOR 1 SPRINGFORM PAN
(8 IN / 20 CM DIAMETER)

♥

FOR THE CRUST:
5.3 oz (150 g) graham crackers, finely crushed
3 tbsp sugar
4 tbsp butter, melted

♥

FOR THE FILLING:
2 cups (450 g) room temperature cream cheese
10.6 oz (300 g) room temperature goat cream cheese
⅓ cup (75 g) room temperature butter
4 eggs
¾ cup + 5 tsp (170 g) sugar
1 vanilla pod

♥

FOR THE FROSTING:
1 cup (250 ml) cream
¾ cup + 2 tbsp (200 g) sour cream
3 tbsp powdered sugar
3 figs
2 tbsp honey

♥

ADDITIONALLY:
Butter for the pan

1. Preheat the oven to 345°F (175°C). Line the springform pan with parchment paper and lightly butter the edges.

2. Mix the crumbled graham crackers, sugar, and melted butter and place on the bottom of the pan. Press down firmly, and bake in the oven for about 15 minutes.

3. For the filling, mix the two types of cream cheese, butter, eggs, sugar and scraped out vanilla pulp from the vanilla pod in a bowl using a hand mixer, until a smooth paste forms. Carefully spread the filling on the crust, and place the cheesecake in the oven for another 35–40 minutes. The center of the cake will appear somewhat soft.

4. Turn off the oven and let the cake cool inside of it, with the door slightly open. (A wooden spoon can be helpful here.) Then store overnight in the refrigerator.

5. For the frosting, before serving, whip the cream, add in sour cream and powdered sugar, and beat to stiff peaks. Spread onto the cake.

6. Cut the figs into quarters and place them on the cake. Drizzle with honey.

JUICY
Applesauce Cake

Applesauce makes this cake so wonderfully juicy, even two days after baking. A real classic on our kitchen counter, where everyone likes to cut a little piece off in passing, until there are only crumbs left on the plate.

FOR 1 BUNDT PAN
(APPROX. 10 IN / 26 CM
DIAMETER, 4 IN / 10 CM HIGH)
2 cups (250 g) flour
1 ½ tsp baking soda
2 tsp cinnamon
2 eggs
1 cup + 2 tbsp (225 g) white sugar
½ cup (100 g) granulated brown
    sugar
1 ¼ cups (360 g) applesauce
    (preferably unsweetened)
⅔ cup (160 ml) vegetable oil

♥

ADDITIONALLY:
Butter and flour for the pan
Powdered sugar for sprinkling

1. Preheat the oven to 345°F (175°C). Butter the bundt pan and sprinkle it with flour.

2. Mix the flour, baking soda, salt, and cinnamon in a bowl, then set aside. In another bowl beat the eggs with the two types of sugar until creamy. Then stir in applesauce and oil.

3. Fold in the flour mixture very gently, making sure not to stir it too much. All ingredients should be just barely just mixed together. Fill the prepared pan with the dough and bake in the oven for about 45 minutes.

4. Let the cake cool in the pan and then flip over onto a cake plate.

5. Before serving, sprinkle with powdered sugar.

Gâteau de Crêpes

WITH VANILLA CREAM AND RASPBERRIES

This cake is also called "Mille Crêpes," which literally means "a thousand thin pancakes." I'm kind of glad there were not quite so many. Yes, you have to stand at the stove for a little while, and flip over very thin pancakes. But the effort is worthwhile, because the cake, with vanilla cream and raspberries, not only looks very picturesque, but tastes just as great.

MAKES 1 GÂTEAU DE CRÊPES

♥

FOR THE DOUGH:
6 eggs
1 pinch salt
2 tbsp sugar
1 ½ cups (350 ml) milk
1 ½ cups + 1 tsp (190 g) flour

♥

FOR THE FILLING:
1 ¼ cups (300 ml) cream
1 tbsp sour cream
1 tbsp powdered sugar
Vanilla pulp, scraped out of 1 pod

♥

ADDITIONALLY:
Vegetable oil for frying
Raspberries and powdered
    sugar for decoration

1. For the dough, mix the eggs with salt and sugar in a bowl. Alternate adding flour and milk. Then let the dough rest for at least ½ hour.

2. In a small pan, heat up some oil, and over medium heat, put 3 tablespoons of batter into the center. Spread out thinly and bake the crepe for 1 minute. Flip over and continue baking for ½ minute. Then remove from the pan, and place onto a plate. Continue making the crepes in this way, until all of the batter is used up. Let the crepes cool down.

3. For the filling, whip the cream, add in sour cream, powdered sugar, and vanilla pulp, and continue beating.

4. Now start building the tower: Lay one crepe on a cake plate, and spread 1 tablespoon of vanilla cream on top. Then alternate adding the crepes and the cream filling in successive layers until the end, when only the most beautiful crepe remains, as the crowning glory. Place this one on top, garnish the cake with raspberries, and sprinkle with powdered sugar.

MY TIP

The cake should be stored in the refrigerator until it is ready to be consumed.

FROM THE
Cookie Jar

I wish my beautiful white display cabinet would always be equipped with an
array of treats, especially jars containing many varieties of cookies. But as soon
as the smell of cookies wafts out of the oven, the baked goods are eaten just
as they are, with only a few making it into a cute little cookie jar, if any.
The fingers of my cookie-loving family are simply too fast.

Coconut Cookies

What do I remember from my trip to the Kurumba Maldives? That these cookies tasted really good, pure and natural, just by themselves. But there also is no reason not to dip them in chocolate before eating them, or pour lemon icing over them. Every time these coconut cookies come out of my oven, I think of these options; however, the cookies are never around long enough for me to implement these ideas. Next time, for sure.

MAKES APPROX. 16 COCONUT COOKIES
(depending on the size)
2 cups (150 g) coconut flakes
½ cup + 1 tsp (120 g) room
   temperature butter
1 ¼ cups (250 g) sugar
2 eggs
2 ⅓ cups (300 g) flour

1. Preheat the oven to 355°F (180°C). Line two baking sheets with parchment paper. If you only have one baking sheet, just bake two batches of cookies, one after another.

2. Put 4 tablespoons of grated coconut in a shallow dish and set aside.

3. Mix butter, sugar and eggs in a bowl. Add the remaining coconut flakes, and then the flour. Now, take this dough (that can still be a bit sticky), and remove pieces of it a tablespoon at a time. Form each tablespoon into a ball. Then roll them in the set-aside coconut flakes.

4. Place approx. 8 little balls on each baking sheet, making sure to place them far enough away from each other, and press flat, so that they are small, 4-cm-wide discs. Bake the cookies for about 18 minutes in the oven.

5. Let cool, and follow the same process for the rest of the coconut cookies.

Baci di dama

The name for these Italian cookies, when translated, is "women's kisses." I think the one who invented this delicious recipe really deserved *mille baci* from all of the women in the world.

MAKES APPROX. 30 BACIS

♥

FOR THE DOUGH:
½ cup (50 g) ground almonds
1 tbsp sugar
1 ½ cups (190 g) flour
½ cup (40 g) unsweetened
    high-quality cocoa powder
¼ tsp baking powder
½ tsp salt
1 cup (230 g) room temperature
    butter
⅔ cup (125 g) powdered sugar
1 tbsp rum

♥

FOR THE FILLING:
8 oz (225 g) chocolate (at least
    70% cocoa content), coarsely
    chopped
1 tbsp butter
¾ cup (175 ml) cream

1. Preheat the oven to 320°F (160°C). Line a baking sheet with parchment paper.

2. For the dough, grind the almonds along with the sugar together until they look like wet sand. Mix flour, cocoa powder, baking powder, and salt in a bowl, then set aside.

3. Beat the butter and powdered sugar in a bowl with a hand mixer until light and creamy. Then add the flour mixture, and finally the ground almonds and rum. Combine everything into a smooth dough, and leave it, wrapped in plastic wrap, in the refrigerator for about 1 hour.

4. Divide the dough into three parts. Put two-thirds of dough back in the refrigerator, and shape the other third into a thin roll (¾ in / 2 cm in diameter). Slice ½-in (1.2 cm) thick pieces from this roll, and form these pieces into balls. Place on the baking sheet and bake for 12–15 minutes. Proceed with the other pieces of dough in the same way. Let the cookies cool down after baking.

5. For the filling, place chocolate and butter in a heatproof bowl. Heat the cream in a saucepan until boiling, and then pour over the chocolate. Let stand briefly, and then stir until the chocolate is shiny and smooth. Allow to cool, and then pour into a piping bag with a round tip.

6. For each baci, spread chocolate filling on the flat side of a cookie and place a second cookie on top.

FRUITY
Sandwich Cookies

My promise: Everyone will like them. Why? Because everyone can hide their favorite jam in between two cookies. So grab a spoon, get set, go.

MAKES 20–30 COOKIES
(depending on the size of the cookie cutter)
2 cups (250 g) flour
½ tsp baking powder
1 pinch salt
¾ cup (170 g) room temperature butter
1 cup + 2 tbsp (225 g) sugar
1 egg
Your favorite marmalade, for spreading on the cookies

♥

ADDITIONALLY:
Powdered sugar for garnishing

1. Mix the flour, baking powder, and salt in a bowl, then set aside.

2. Cream the butter and sugar with a hand mixer. Add in the egg, and then slowly mix in the flour mixture. From that, form a smooth dough, preferably with your hands, and divide it into two portions. Wrap the dough in plastic wrap and leave it in the refrigerator for 1 hour.

3. Preheat the oven to 375°F (190°C). Line two baking sheets with parchment paper (or if you don't have two baking sheets, just bake one batch after another).

4. Now roll out the dough thinly, and cut out circles from that, using a cookie cutter or floured glasses. Cut out little shapes from one of the two sides of the sandwich cookies, if desired, and place everything on the baking sheet. Keep in the oven for 8–10 minutes.

5. After cooling, spread one half of a sandwich cookie with your favorite jam, and place a second half on top. Garnish with powdered sugar.

Snickerdoodles

Nomen est omen. If someone writes a blog called *Sugar, Cinnamon, and Love*, that must mean they love snickerdoodles. Sugar and cinnamon play the main roles in this classic American cookie. And a whole lot more *amore* is added when you roll the little balls yourself, cover them in the cinnamon sugar, put them onto the baking sheet, and count down the 8 minutes of the baking time.

MAKES APPROX. 30
SNICKERDOODLES

¾ cup + 5 tbsp (170 g) white sugar

⅔ cup (130 g) granulated
    brown sugar

½ cup (115 g) room temperature
    butter

1 egg

1 ½ cups (185 g) flour

1 tsp baking powder

1–2 tsp cinnamon

1 pinch salt

♥

FOR THE CINNAMON SUGAR
COATING:

6 tbsp (75 g) sugar

1 ½ tsp cinnamon

1. Preheat the oven to 390°F (200°C).

2. Cream both types of sugar and the butter in a bowl with the hand mixer. Then add the egg.

3. Mix the flour, baking powder, cinnamon, and salt, add those ingredients to the butter mixture, and combine everything into a smooth dough. Roll into 30 balls.

4. For the coating, mix sugar and cinnamon in a small bowl. Roll the balls around in this mixture and place on a baking sheet lined with parchment paper, leaving some space between the balls. They may roll around a little, so make sure that they are not directly next to each other after putting them in the oven. If not all of the balls fit on the baking sheet, use two baking sheets or bake in two batches.

5. Bake the Snickerdoodles for about 8 minutes in the oven, then let cool.

Cinnamon Roll Cookies

These cookies look like little carousels, in which sugar and cinnamon swirled properly through the dough and into a sweet pastry. My ode to cinnamon buns in a new, handy cookie format.

MAKES APPROX. 30 CINNAMON
ROLL COOKIES
(depending on the size)

♥

FOR THE DOUGH:
½ cup + 1 tbsp (125 g) room
    temperature butter
⅔ cup (120 g) sugar
2 tsp (8 g) vanilla sugar
1 egg
2 cups (250 g) flour
1 tsp baking powder
1 egg white, whisked together
    with 1 tbsp water
¼ cup (50 g) sugar
1 tsp cinnamon

♥

FOR THE ICING:
⅔ cup (75 g) powdered sugar
1 tbsp milk

♥

ADDITIONALLY:
Flour for the countertop

1. Preheat the oven to 345°F (175°C). Line a baking sheet with parchment paper.

2. Beat the butter, sugar and vanilla sugar in a bowl with a hand mixer until creamy.

3. Stir in the egg. Then mix the flour and baking powder, and add them in. Knead with your hands into a smooth dough. Then shape into a ball, wrap in plastic wrap, and keep in the refrigerator for 1 hour.

4. Roll the dough out thinly on the floured countertop, into a rectangle. Brush with egg white and sprinkle with sugar and cinnamon. Then gently, tightly roll up, starting with the long side. (The dough may be sticky, so roll it out gently.) Re-wrap in plastic wrap and refrigerate for 15–30 minutes. Then cut into slices and place on the baking paper. If not all of the cinnamon roll cookies can fit on the baking sheet, bake in two batches, one right after another.

5. Bake the cinnamon roll cookies for 8–10 minutes in the oven. Then leave to cool.

6. Make icing by mixing powdered sugar and milk together, and decorate the cookies with that.

Strawberry Cookies

Strawberries are a wonder of nature. At least once every summer we go to a strawberry farm and collect these gems until we have two huge baskets full (quite a few strawberries also went straight into our mouths). There were several competitions on these trips: Who can find the biggest strawberry? Who can find the smallest, reddest or who the funniest one? Then we go home, and I preheat the oven. Because in this case, baking just has to happen . . . .

MAKES 16 COOKIES

1 ⅓ cups (170 g) flour

3 tsp baking powder

2 tsp cinnamon

½ cup (110 g) room temperature butter

⅔ cup (120 g) granulated brown sugar

1 cup (240 ml) milk

10.5 oz (300 g) strawberries, washed and diced finely

1. Preheat the oven to 375°F (190°C). Line a baking sheet with parchment paper.

2. Mix flour, baking powder and cinnamon in a bowl. Work in the butter until the mixture is crumbly. Then mix with the sugar.

3. Add in the milk, and knead the strawberries under, very gently. Combine everything into a smooth dough.

4. Using a tablespoon, place approx. 16 dough circles on a baking sheet and bake in the oven for 20 minutes.

Raspberry Sugar Palmiers

We all know them from our grandmothers. Well, back then we called them pigs ears, and they were larger, and not created with fine raspberry sugar. However, from years back to today, they have always tasted absolutely delicious.

MAKES APPROX. 15 PALMIERS
(depending on the desired thickness)
1 roll of puff pastry from the refrigerated section (not frozen!)
6 tbsp sugar
2 tbsp freeze-dried raspberries
1 tbsp butter, melted

1. Get 1 puff pastry out of the refrigerator and leave at room temperature briefly, otherwise cracks and wrinkles form easily.

2. Grind sugar and dried raspberries very finely with the food processor.

3. Roll out the puff pastry and brush with melted butter. Then sprinkle evenly with the raspberry sugar and lightly tap (the back of a tablespoon can help here) to ensure the sugar stays on.

4. Now roll the puff pastry tightly from both sides, so that two rolls meet in the middle. Wrap well in plastic wrap and refrigerate for ½ hour. Meanwhile, preheat the oven to 390°F (200°C).

5. Quickly cut the roll of dough with a very sharp knife into ⅓-in (1 cm) thick slices. Place these, at a distance from each other, on a baking sheet lined with parchment paper (or two baking sheets, depending on the amount of dough and size of the baking sheet) and bake for approx. 10 minutes in the oven. The Palmiers should only brown slightly, otherwise they become crispy and firm.

MY TIP

If desired, after baking, the Palmiers can be coated in icing or chocolate, or can be dipped in espresso and eaten quickly.

Pie Fries

WITH SUGAR, CINNAMON, AND LOVE

The next time you hear "Maaama, when are we having fries again?" try making these. I'm sure the kids will love them. If I have leftover dough after baking a pie, it will always be turned in to pie fries. A delicious recycling.

MAKES APPROX. 60 PIE FRIES
(depending on the desired size)
1 ⅔ cups (200 g) flour
1 pinch salt
½ tsp sugar
½ cup (105 g) very cold butter, cut
    into pieces
⅓ cup (80 ml) ice cold water

ADDITIONALLY:
Flour for the countertop
⅓ cup (60 g) sugar
1 tbsp cinnamon (or a little more or
    less, depending on your tastes)

MY TIP

1. Mix the flour, salt and sugar. Add the butter and mix quickly in a food processor until the pieces of butter have become pea-sized. Don't knead for too long!

2. Add water and mix until the dough just starts to hold together.

3. Quickly shape the dough into a disc (do not knead) and keep in the refrigerator for about 40 minutes, wrapped in plastic wrap.

4. Preheat the oven to 345°F (175°C). Line a baking sheet with parchment paper.

5. Roll out the dough on a lightly floured surface (keep turning occasionally, so it does not stick to the work surface). Then use a pizza cutter (or a dough cutter), cut into fries, sprinkle generously with sugar and cinnamon, and place onto the prepared baking sheet. Bake 15–20 minutes in the oven. Then allow to cool.

Depending on your taste, the pie fries can be dipped into jam, fruit puree, applesauce, caramel or chocolate cream.

Cherry and Hazelnut
COOKIES

This is a cookie for all nut lovers. And I have at least two of those at my house. But since I also love fruit, I created this hazelnut cookie recipe with cherries. One could say, therefore, that this cookie is our "family consensus cookie."

MAKES APPROX. 20 COOKIES
2 ⅓ cups (300 g) flour
¼ tsp baking soda
1 pinch salt
1 cup (230 g) room temperature butter
1 cup (180 g) sugar
1 egg
1 handful freeze-dried cherries
2.1 oz (60 g) sliced hazelnuts, plus a few extra for garnishing

♥

FOR THE ICING:
1 tbsp milk
⅔ cup (75 g) powdered sugar

1. Preheat the oven to 345°F (175°C). Line a baking sheet with parchment paper.

2. Mix the flour, baking soda, and salt in a bowl, then set aside.

3. Cream butter and sugar in another bowl. Add the egg, and then mix for about 2 minutes, using a hand mixer.

4. First add the flour mixture, and then the dried cherries and hazelnuts. Mix everything together well.

5. Place the dough, in walnut-sized pieces, on the parchment paper, each sprinkled with a few extra hazelnuts, and bake 20–25 minutes in the oven.

6. Let cool on a baking rack. Mix milk and powdered sugar to make the icing, spread it on the cookies, and garnish with a few more hazelnut slices.

Almond Balls

These round little almond cookies are somewhat reminiscent of German crescent Christmas cookies. But no one will keep you from enjoying these soft buttery almond cookies in the spring, summer or fall—and without jingles belling in the background, or an O-Christmas tree getting decorated with colorful ornaments.

MAKES APPROX. 20 ALMOND BALLS
(depending on the size)
1 ½ cups (345 g) room temperature butter
¾ cup (90 g) powdered sugar
½ tsp salt
1 ½ cups + 1 tbsp (150 g) finely ground almonds
3 cups (375 g) flour

♥

ADDITIONALLY:
⅔ cup (75 g) powdered sugar, to toss the cookies in

1. Preheat the oven to 320°F (160°C). Line a baking sheet with parchment paper.

2. Beat the butter and powdered sugar in a bowl until creamy. Add salt, and mix with a hand mixer until the mixture becomes light and fluffy.

3. Add the almonds, and then gradually add the flour. Combine everything into a smooth dough.

4. Now take walnut-sized pieces from the dough, form balls with your hands, and place onto the baking sheet. Press down on each ball gently.

5. Bake the almond balls for 15–20 minutes in the oven.

6. Remove the cookies from the oven and allow to cool for 2–3 minutes. Then roll them in powdered sugar, and let cool completely.

Chocolate Walnut

COOKIES

An integral part of coffee shops: chocolate chip cookies (here with walnuts). This cookie is a true classic, and everyone chases after the perfect recipe. Here's mine, which our cookie jar often houses. But of course, not for too long.

MAKES APPROX. 28 COOKIES

⅔ cup (150 g) room temperature
  butter
⅓ cup + 1 tbsp (80 g) white sugar
⅓ cup + 1 tbsp (80 g) granulated
  brown sugar
1 egg
1 ¾ cups + 1 tbsp (225 g) flour
½ tsp baking soda
1 pinch salt
7 oz (200 g) chocolate, chopped
1 handful walnuts, chopped

1. Preheat the oven to 375°F (190°C). Line two baking sheets with parchment paper.

2. Mix the butter and both types of sugar in a bowl with a hand mixer until creamy. Add the egg.

3. Sift flour, baking soda, and salt, and add in. Mix everything together with a spoon. Add chocolate and walnuts, and mix everything together well.

4. Using a small spoon, take pieces of dough that are about 1 ½ in (4 cm) high and place them on the parchment paper, making sure to leave a sufficient distance between them. Warning, the cookies will spread out during baking and become larger! So preferably, bake in 2 subsequent batches with not too many cookies on one baking sheet.

5. Place the cookies in the oven and let bake for 8–10 minutes. The cookies should not be too hard, as they continue to harden after baking. Allow to cool briefly, seal up in an airtight container, and store, preferably hidden away from cookie monsters.

Dulce de Leche

I love dulce de leche, a milk spread from the Latin American region, on rice pudding, ice cream or bananas. Now it's connected in the tastiest and creamiest way with these cookies to make a dreamy cookie sandwich.

MAKES APPROX. 15 SANDWICH
COOKIES

1 cup (225 g) room temperature
    butter
⅓ cup (70 g) sugar
1 pinch salt
2 ½ cups (310 g) flour
1 tbsp rum
3.5 oz (100 g) walnuts, finely chopped
2 cups + 1 tbsp (250 g) powdered
    sugar
5.3 oz (150 g) Dulce de Leche or
caramel cream

1. Mix the butter, sugar and salt in a bowl. Then add the flour, and knead everything for 1–2 minutes. Add the rum and walnuts as well.

2. Now divide the dough into two pieces. Roll each piece of dough into a 1 ¼-in (3 cm) thick roll. Cut into small slices (about ¼ in or ½ cm wide), and place on a baking sheet lined with parchment paper. Let the cookies cool for about ½ hour.

3. Preheat the oven to 340°F (170°C). Get the powdered sugar ready in a small bowl. Bake the cookies for 20 minutes in the oven. When they come out, immediately roll in powdered sugar, and let cool on a wire rack.

4. Then spread dulce de leche or caramel cream on half of the cookies, and put the remaining cookies on top.

MY TIP

For those who want to make dulce de leche themselves: Preheat oven to 430°F (220°C). Put sweetened condensed milk from the supermarket in a baking dish and cover with aluminum foil. Then place this into an even bigger baking dish, and fill with about ¾ in (2 cm) of boiling water, and let cook in the oven for about 1 ½ hours. Then either use the cooled caramel cream filling right away, or store in the refrigerator.

French Tarts
AND
American Pies

Why do I love tarts and pies so much? Only a few recipes can, by changing just the main ingredients, create so much variation, magic and deliciousness. From whatever you can find at the market, or in the fruit basket, plus only a few ingredients, you can create a celebration of the season. Simple and full of flavor, just like I like it.

Nectarine Pistachio
FRANGIPANE

This tart is probably one of the most demanded and repeatedly baked recipes in my repertoire. The play of colors from the orange and red fruits, the crunchy brown of the tart, and green pistachios is fantastic. This pastry is also very easy to make, and tastes so wonderful in late summer.

MAKES 1 FRANGIPANE

1 ⅔ cups (150 g) slivered almonds

1.4 oz (40 g) unsalted pistachios
  without shells

¾ cup (150 g) sugar

¼ tsp salt

2 eggs, whisked

2 tbsp butter, melted

1 tsp vanilla extract

Almond flavoring, to taste

1 roll puff pastry from the
  refrigerated section (not frozen!)

3–4 nectarines, washed and cut
  into wedges

♥

ADDITIONALLY:

1 tbsp chopped pistachios and
  slivered almonds for garnishing

1 tbsp granulated brown sugar for
  sprinkling

1. Preheat the oven to 320°F (160°C). Then distribute the slivered almonds and pistachios evenly on a baking sheet and roast in the oven for about 10 minutes.

2. Grind the almonds and pistachios finely, preferably in a food processor. Then add sugar and salt, and continue to grind. Add eggs, butter, and vanilla extract, and then almond extract to taste. Mix everything into a spreadable cream.

3. Unroll the puff pastry and trim into a circle. Poke holes evenly across the dough with a fork, fold down the edges (making sure to press the corners together, so that everything holds together well), and bake for 8 minutes on a baking sheet lined with parchment paper. The baking sheet should be in the top third of the oven, and the oven should be heated to 430°F (220°C). Once the tart is out of the oven, briefly let it sit. Turn the oven temperature down to 355°F (180°C).

4. Spread a thin layer of the pistachio-almond cream onto the crust.

5. Place the nectarine slices across the whole tart in a fan shape. Garnish with pistachios and almonds, sprinkle with granulated brown sugar, and then bake for 35–40 minutes.

Cherry and Hazelnut
GALETTES

When I stroll around the weekly market very early in the morning, and see thick red cherries gazing back at me, I cannot resist buying them and baking something fantastic. For example, these very simple French galettes.

MAKES 4 SMALL GALETTES:
(6 IN / 15 CM DIAMETER)

♥

FOR THE PÂTE BRISÉE
(FRENCH SHORTCRUST PASTRY):

2 ½ cups (310 g) flour

2 tsp sugar

1 tsp salt

1 cup (230 g) very cold butter, in pieces

¼ cup (60 ml) ice cold water

♥

FOR THE FILLING:

4 tbsp ground hazelnuts

2 handfuls dark cherries, pitted

1 egg white, whisked together with 1 tbsp milk

5 tbsp granulated brown sugar

1. For the dough, mix flour, sugar and salt. Add in the cold butter, and quickly knead with your hands. Gradually add the ice cold water, and then knead until the dough just barely holds together. If it is too dry, add a little bit of water, a teaspoon at a time, and work into the dough well.

2. Press the dough slightly flat and wrap in plastic wrap. Refrigerate for at least 1 hour (3 days at maximum).

3. Then take the dough out of the refrigerator, and let it sit out for 10 minutes. Next, divide it into 4 pieces and roll each piece into a small disc (6 in / 15 cm diameter). Place onto two baking sheets lined with parchment paper, making sure to leave enough distance between the discs.

4. Sprinkle each galette with 1 tbsp ground hazelnuts, and place the pitted cherries in the middle. Leave ¾ in (2 cm) around the edge of the dough without fruit or nuts, fold that part towards the center, and press down firmly. Then brush with beaten egg whites.

5. Now sprinkle the galettes with granulated brown sugar. Place in the refrigerator again for ½ hour. Meanwhile, preheat the oven to 390°F (200°C).

6. Bake the galettes for about ½ hour in the oven. Afterwards, reduce the temperature to 375°F (190°C) and bake for another 10–15 minutes. Enjoy, preferably when they are just out of the oven and still warm.

MY TIP

Whoever wants to can dust the galettes with powdered sugar or serve with vanilla ice cream—that out of sheer joy, will melt away immediately over the warm cherries.

Light Lemon Tart

I love the subtle sweetness of this tart. A little sour, a bit sweet, but very fine and almost as light as a feather. Does my scale see that in the same way? It does not matter. My heart for the kitchen is getting bigger and the summery joy I feel when eating this tart is fabulous.

FOR 1 TART PAN WITH REMOVABLE BOTTOM, ALTERNATIVE: 1 SPRINGFORM PAN (9 ½ IN / 24 CM DIAMETER)

♥

FOR THE SHORTCRUST PASTRY:
1 ½ cups (180 g) flour
¼ cup (50 g) powdered sugar
⅓ cup (30 g) ground almonds without skin
½ cup +1 tbsp (125 g) cold butter, cut into pieces
1 egg yolk

♥

FOR THE FILLING:
½ cup + 1 tsp (125 ml) fresh lemon juice
Zest from 1 organic lemon
5 eggs
¾ cup (150 g) sugar
1 ¼ cups (300 g) heavy cream

♥

ADDITIONALLY:
Beans for blind baking
Powdered sugar for garnishing

1. For the crust, rub flour, powdered sugar, almonds and butter well with your hands, until crumbly. Then add the egg yolk, and mix everything together quickly, into a smooth dough. Press flat and keep cold for at least 1 hour.

2. Take the dough out of the refrigerator, and let it sit out at room temperature for 10 minutes. Then roll it out so that it covers the edges of the tart pan. Pour the mixture into the mold and keep cold for another ½ hour.

3. Preheat the oven to 390°F (200°C), using top and bottom heat.

4. Lay out parchment paper on the bottom of the tart pan (but on top of the dough), fill the pan with beans and blind bake for 10 minutes. Then, remove the parchment paper and beans, and bake for another 10 minutes. Take the tart out of the oven, let it cool, and reduce the oven temperature to 320°F (160°C).

5. For the filling, mix lemon juice, zest, eggs, sugar, and heavy cream in a bowl, and stir well with a whisk. Then pass the mixture through a fine sieve and pour carefully onto the prepared crust. Bake the tart for 40 minutes. Then sprinkle with powdered sugar and enjoy.

Engadine Nut Cake

This Engadine nut cake, or "Tuorta da Nusch" is a culinary dream for nut lovers! No compromises. Pure nuts. You crack when trying to cut into them, they crack when you bite into them. Those who travel to Canton will find the top-secret variants of this cake in many bakeries and pastry shops.

FOR 1 SPRINGFORM PAN
(9 ½ IN / 24 CM DIAMETER)

♥

FOR THE DOUGH:
2 ⅓ cups + 1 tsp (300 g) flour
¾ cup (150 g) sugar
⅔ cup (150 g) cold butter, cut
    into pieces
1 egg
1 pinch salt

♥

FOR THE FILLING:
1 ½ cups (300 g) sugar
14 oz (400 g) walnuts, coarsely
    chopped (or 7 oz / 200 g
    walnuts and 7 oz / 200 g
    hazelnuts)
¾ cup + 4 tsp (200 ml) cream

♥

ADDITIONALLY:
Butter and flour for the pan

1. Butter the pan and sprinkle with flour.

2. For the dough, knead flour, sugar, and butter. Then, add the egg and the salt, and form the dough into a ball. Chill for approximately ½ hour.

3. Roll out two-thirds of the dough and place it in the baking pan. Form a crust out of it, making sure to pull the dough up around the edges, and put it in the refrigerator again for ½ hour.

4. Meanwhile, preheat the oven to 345°F (175°C).

5. For the filling, heat the sugar in a pot and let caramelize until it is light brown. Then add the nuts, and finally pour in the cream. Stir continuously. Boil the mixture until the caramel has dissolved.

6. Distribute the filling on top of the crust. Roll out the rest of the dough, and use as a cover over the filling, pressing the edges together well. Alternatively, you can cut out little hearts from the dough and place in slightly overlapping layers on top of the nut mixture.

7. Bake the cake for ½ hour in the oven. Reduce the temperature to 300°F (150°C) and continue baking for 10–15 minutes.

This nut cake tastes best once it has sat out for one day.

MY TIP

114

Vanilla Pear Tartlets
WITH MARZIPAN

If you ask me if I'm more of a pear or an apple type, I would have, until recently, very determinedly cried out "Apple apple apple!" But after I baked these tartlets, I have to revise something. On top of dough, pears are a dream, and I have probably just been doing them wrong for many years. From now on, I am an apple AND pear type of person.

MAKES 6 TARTLETS
3 small pears
Juice from ½ lemon
1 vanilla pod
1 cup (200 g) sugar
1 roll puff pastry from the
    refrigerated section (not frozen!)
3.5 oz (100 g) marzipan,
    coarsely grated

♥

ADDITIONALLY:
Powdered sugar for sprinkling

1. Preheat the oven to 355°F (180°C). Line a baking sheet with parchment paper and set aside.

2. Peel the pears (the stems may stay on, I think they're very pretty), cut in half lengthwise and squeeze some lemon juice onto them immediately. Cut open the vanilla pod, and scrape out the pulp.

3. In a pot, combine 2 cups (450 ml) of water, sugar, vanilla pulp and the scraped out vanilla pod, and heat until the sugar has dissolved. Place the pears in the pot and let cook for about 5 minutes. Then remove, and let cool.

4. Then remove the seeds from the pears with a small spoon. Cut into them, but not all the way through, so you can fan them out, but they are still connected to each other at the upper end.

5. Get the puffed pastry out of the refrigerator and allow it to sit out at room temperature for about 10 minutes. Roll out, and cut out 6 circles that are slightly larger than the pear halves. Put the dough circles on a baking sheet and sprinkle with grated marzipan. Put the pear halves on top, lightly fan out (using a flat hand and gentle pressure works great), and bake for about 20 minutes in the oven.

6. Then quickly sprinkle with powdered sugar and let caramelize in the oven (preferably on the broil setting) for 2 minutes. Then remove from the oven.

MY TIP

These tartlets are best enjoyed topped with maple syrup, vanilla ice cream or lightly whipped cream and cinnamon.

Linzer Star Tart

A magnificent classic that you can decorate with different shapes for many special occasions, or simply place weaved strips of dough on top: My personal starry sky of raspberry and hazelnut.

FOR 1 SPRINGFORM PAN
(9 ½ IN / 24 CM DIAMETER)
2 cups (250 g flour)
1 pinch cinnamon
1 pinch salt
1 cup + 1 ⅔ tbsp (250 g) room
   temperature butter
1 ¼ cups (250 g) sugar
8.8 oz (250 g) ground hazelnuts
Zest from 1 organic lemon
¾ cup (250 g) raspberry
   marmalade

♥

ADDITIONALLY:
Whipped cream as desired

1. Mix the flour, cinnamon and salt in a bowl, then set aside.

2. In another bowl, cream the butter and sugar, and then add ground hazelnuts and lemon zest.

3. Add in the flour mixture, and knead everything together, but only until the dough just barely holds together.

4. Then press it flat, wrap it in plastic wrap and place it in the refrigerator for 1 hour.

5. Preheat the oven to 345°F (175°C).

6. Roll out approx. ⅔ of the dough, put it into a springform pan, and form a crust, being sure to pull up the edges.

7. Then fill evenly with raspberry jam. Roll out the remaining dough and cut it into whatever shapes you desire. Place these dough shapes on top of the raspberry jam, and bake the tart for about 40 minutes in the oven.

8. Let cool and enjoy with a splash of cream.

Tarte Tatin

WITH APRICOTS AND ROSEMARY

This tart is a French classic that allegedly arose by chance in the 19th century, when the Tatin sisters wanted to bake an apple pie and a little mishap occurred: The apple pie shifted out of place, and lay in the pan in the wrong way, but was baked just like that. Since then, there has been a new tart in the world, "Tarte du chef" or "Tarte des demoiselles Tatin," as it is often called, and not only in France. Let's hear it for this mishap, otherwise we might still be living without these delicious caramelized reverse tarts.

MAKES 1 TART

⅔ cup (120 g) sugar

1 ⅓ tbsp (20 g) butter

2 sprigs rosemary

6–8 apricot halves (1 can), dried very well

1 roll puff pastry from the refrigerated section (not frozen!)

♥

ADDITIONALLY:

Crème fraîche, whipped cream or vanilla ice cream, as desired

1. Preheat the oven to 480°F (250°C).

2. Caramelize sugar in a medium-sized, oven-safe skillet for about 4 minutes on the stove over medium heat.

3. Add butter and rosemary, and then put the apricots with the cut side up in the pan. Then take the pan off the heat.

4. Cut circles out of the puff pastry, with a diameter that is slightly larger than the pan. Now place the dough on top of the apricots and push the edges under the fruit using a knife. Do this carefully, as the caramelized sugar is very hot!

5. Now place the pan in the oven and bake the tart for 15–20 minutes. Then, after leaving it out at room temperature for a short time, remove the tart from the pan by turning it upside down and gently letting it fall out onto a large plate.

6. Serve with crème fraîche or vanilla ice cream.

Chocolate Cream

HAZELNUT TART

I confess, we never go without chocolate spread in our household. Even my husband and my son (in that order) make sure that we pick up a reserve jar when shopping. Here is the result of the use of this cream, in baking: a wonderfully nutty, and just as creamy, tart.

FOR 1 TART PAN (9 ½ IN / 24 CM DIAMETER)

♥

FOR THE CRUST:
1 ⅔ cups (200 g) flour
1 pinch salt
1 tsp sugar
½ cup (100 g) very cold butter, cut into pieces
⅓ cup (80 ml) ice cold water

♥

FOR THE FILLING:
2 tbsp cornstarch
2 cups (470 ml) cream
5 oz (140 g) chocolate spread
1 pinch salt
1 pinch cinnamon
3.5 oz (100 g) hazelnuts, coarsely chopped

♥

ADDITIONALLY:
Beans for blind baking

1. For the dough, mix flour, salt and sugar together. Add the butter, and stir everything together rapidly, until the mixture is crumbly.

2. Add the water, and combine everything (quickly again) into a dough. If it is too dry, add a little bit of water, a tablespoon at a time, until it holds together.

3. Wrap the dough in plastic wrap and refrigerate for at least ½ hour.

4. Preheat the oven to 345°F (175°C).

5. Remove the dough from the refrigerator, press into a tart pan with a removable bottom, creating an even crust. Remove the leftover dough from along the edges, and poke the bottom with a fork. Cover with parchment paper and fill with beans. Blind bake for 20 minutes in the oven and let cool. Remove beans and parchment paper.

6. For the filling, mix ¼ cup (60 ml) of cream with the cornstarch. In a pot, mix the rest of the cream with the chocolate spread, salt, and cinnamon thoroughly. Then add in the starch mixture. Bring to a boil and let thicken, while stirring, until a pudding-like consistency results. Then allow to cool.

7. Spread the filling on the bottom of the tart, and bake in the oven at 300°F (150°C), using top and bottom heat for 25–30 minutes. Then allow to cool, and place in the refrigerator for about 4 hours. Before serving sprinkle with hazelnuts.

Banana Tartlets

WITH DULCE DE LECHE

Homemade dulce de leche can not only be used on cookies (see p. 104), but also in this case as a soft, sweet bed for bananas, that together with whipped cream is set into this cute little nest of a tartlet. These ingredients together make up a great tart team.

MAKES 6 SMALL TARTLETS
OR 1 LARGE TART
(9 IN / 23 CM DIAMETER)

♥

FOR THE CRUST:

1 ⅔ cups (200 g) flour

1 pinch salt

1 tsp sugar

½ cup (100 g) very cold butter, cut
   into pieces

⅓ cup (80 ml) ice cold water

♥

FOR THE FILLING:

1 can sweetened condensed milk
   (14 oz / 400 g)

3 bananas, peeled and cut into
   slices

⅔ cup + 1 tbsp (200 ml) cream

♥

ADDITIONALLY:

Cocoa powder or cinnamon sugar
   for garnishing

1. Sift the flour, salt and sugar, and mix together. Cut the butter into pieces, melt it, and mix everything together rapidly until the mixture is crumbly.

2. Add the water and combine everything (again quickly) into a dough. If it is too dry, add water a tablespoon at a time, until it holds together.

3. Wrap the dough in plastic wrap and refrigerate for at least ½ hour.

4. Preheat the oven to 375°F (190°C). Roll out the dough thinly and place it into 6 tartlet pans. Poke the bottom of the dough several times with a fork and bake for 15–20 minutes in the oven. Then let them cool.

5. For the filling, heat the oven to 430°F (220°C). Pour the condensed milk into a baking dish and cover with aluminum foil. Then place this in an even bigger baking dish, and fill that dish ¾ in (2 cm) high with boiling water. Put everything in the oven for 1 ½ hours. Then spread the cooled milk cream on the tartlet crusts.

6. Cut the bananas and lay them on top of the caramel. Beat the cream to stiff peaks and pipe onto the banana slices. Sprinkle the tartlets with cocoa or cinnamon sugar, as desired.

Apple Pie
WITH CRANBERRIES

The apples in this pie caramelize so beautifully in the oven, and along with the cranberries, create a wonderful taste experience. If you still have some vanilla ice cream in the freezer and don't know what to do with it, here is the recipe for that ice cream's perfect companion.

FOR 1 PIE PAN
(9 ½ IN / 24 CM DIAMETER)

♥

FOR THE CRUST:
1 ⅔ cups (200 g) flour
1 pinch salt
1 tsp sugar
½ cup (100 g) very cold butter
⅓ cup (80 ml) ice cold water

♥

FOR THE FILLING:
¾ cup (150 g) granulated brown sugar
3 tbsp flour
1 pinch cinnamon
1 pinch salt
4 apples, peeled, cored and cut into thin slices
1 handful fresh cranberries
1 tbsp butter

♥

ADDITIONALLY:
Granulated brown sugar for sprinkling

1. For the dough, mix flour, salt and sugar. Add the butter in pieces and mix everything rapidly until a crumbly mixture results.

2. Add the water and knead everything (again, quickly) into a dough. If it is too dry, add water a tablespoon at a time, until it holds together.

3. Wrap the dough in plastic wrap and refrigerate for at least ½ hour.

4. Meanwhile, for the filling, mix sugar, flour, cinnamon and salt. Add in the apples and cranberries and mix everything well, until the apples are coated with the sugar mixture.

5. Set the oven to 390°F (200°C).

6. Take the dough out of the refrigerator and with the help of a rolling pin, roll it out in a circle that is a little bit bigger than the pie pan.

7. Place the dough gently into the pan, put the apple slices on top of the dough in a single layer, add small pieces of butter on top of the apples, and sprinkle with granulated brown sugar to taste.

8. Pinch the edges of the dough over the apples and bake the pie for 40–50 minutes in the oven.

Ricotta Orange Tart

Wishing it was summer? Here is a piece of the sunny season in tart format. To keep it fresh, please do not forget to put it in the refrigerator. Also, you'll have to be patient, because cooling must happen directly after baking, so this wonderfully light, subtly sweet ricotta and orange tart can develop its full flavor.

FOR 1 TART PAN WITH
A REMOVABLE BOTTOM
(9 IN / 23 CM DIAMETER)

♥

FOR THE CRUST:
1 ⅔ cups (200 g) flour
1 pinch salt
½ tsp sugar
½ cup (105 g) very cold butter,
    cut into pieces
⅓ cup (80 ml) ice cold water

♥

FOR THE FILLING:
7.4 oz (210 g) ricotta
½ cup (100 g) sugar
½ tbsp flour
½ tbsp zest from 1 organic orange
2 eggs

♥

ADDITIONALLY:
Powdered sugar, for garnishing

1. For the dough, mix flour, salt, and sugar. Add the butter and knead everything together quickly until it is crumbly. Add the water, and form the dough into a ball. Chill for at least ½ hour.

2. Then take the dough out of the fridge, roll it out thinly, and line the tart pan with it. Trim the edges, poke the bottom of the dough several times with a fork and place it in the fridge again.

3. Preheat the oven to 345°F (175°C).

4. For the ricotta filling, mix sugar, flour, and orange zest in a bowl, with a hand mixer, then set aside. Beat the eggs for 5 minutes, until frothy, and then mix well with the ricotta mixture. Remove the pan from the refrigerator and spread the filling evenly over the dough. Then bake the tart in the oven for about 45 minutes (without opening the oven door, even if you're really curious, and your patience is failing as soon as this smell wafts through the kitchen).

5. Allow to cool, then place in the fridge, and shortly before eating, garnish generously with powdered sugar.

Maple Syrup Pecan Pie

Normally, the maple syrup at our house ends up on a stack of delicious pancakes. And that is, for once, my husband's work. Those circular breakfast miracles are something he can simply do better. But this time I have kidnapped the maple syrup and given a wonderful pecan pie a North American touch. A small Indian summer for the kitchen!

FOR 1 PIE PAN
(DIAMETER 9 ½ IN / 24 CM OR
10 ¼ IN / 26 CM)

♥

FOR THE CRUST:
1 ⅔ cups (200 g) flour
1 pinch salt
¼ tsp sugar
7 tbsp very cold butter, cut into
   pieces
⅓ cup (80 ml) ice cold water

♥

FOR THE FILLING:
3 eggs
½ cup + 2 ½ tsp (110 g) sugar
¾ cup (240 ml) maple syrup
3 tbsp butter, melted
1 pinch salt
5.3 oz (150 g) pecan halves

♥

ADDITIONALLY:
Flour for the countertop

1. For the pie dough, mix flour, salt, and sugar. Add the butter, and rub with your hands until crumbly. Then add the water and process everything into a smooth dough. Press slightly flat and keep cold for at least ½ hour.

2. Then roll out the dough on the floured countertop and place into a pie tin. Cut off the protruding edges. Store in the refrigerator.

3. Preheat the oven to 375°F (190°C).

4. Meanwhile, for the filling, beat the eggs and sugar in a bowl until creamy. Add maple syrup, butter, salt, and pecan halves, and mix well.

5. Remove the pie pan from the refrigerator and spread the filling evenly over the bottom. Then bake for about 45 minutes in the oven.

Blueberry Pie

This simple blueberry pie smells and tastes like summer to me. I love the fresh blueberries that bubble so beautifully during baking and color the sugary crust purple.

FOR 1 RECTANGULAR TART PAN
(13 ¾ X 4 ½ IN / 35 X 11 CM,
PREFERABLY WITH A
REMOVABLE BOTTOM)

♥

FOR THE CRUST:
2 ½ cups + 1 tsp (315 g) flour
1 pinch salt
1 tsp sugar
¾ cup + 1 tbsp + 1 tsp (190 g) very
   cold butter, cut into pieces
½ cup + 1 tsp (125 ml) ice cold
   water

♥

FOR THE FILLING:
17.6 oz (500 g) blueberries (fresh or
   frozen, not thawed)
⅔ cup (150 g) sugar
3 tbsp cornstarch
1 pinch cinnamon
Zest from 1 organic lemon
1 tbsp lemon juice
1 egg, whisked
A little bit of brown granulated
   sugar

1. Mix the flour, salt, and sugar. Add the butter and mix everything rapidly into a crumbly mixture.

2. Add the water and combine everything (quickly again) into a dough. If it is too dry, add a tablespoon of water at a time, until it holds together.

3. Divide the dough into two equal pieces and lightly press flat. Wrap in plastic wrap and refrigerate for at least ½ hour.

4. Then roll out a piece of the dough thinly and put in a tart pan, cutting off the excess edges. Poke holes in the dough with a fork and place the pan in the refrigerator.

5. Set the oven to 375°F (190°C).

6. In the meantime, to make the filling, mix the blueberries with sugar, cornstarch, cinnamon, lemon zest, and lemon juice, and let stand for 10 minutes. Next, take the prepared pan out of the refrigerator and pour in the blueberry mixture. Then chill again.

7. In the meantime, roll out the second portion of dough and cut out different shapes with a small cookie cutter. Place the dough carefully on top of the blueberry filling and cut off the edges.

8. Now brush the pie with egg, sprinkle with granulated brown sugar, and bake for 50–60 minutes in the oven. Let cool for 1 hour, and then enjoy.

Strawberry Pie

WITH CRÈME FRAÎCHE

This is a pie to make when you want to enjoy a day off from the oven. Because this fresh strawberry dream is instead prepared in the refrigerator, before making its grand entrance.

FOR 1 PIE PAN OR SPRINGFORM
PAN (8 IN / 20 CM DIAMETER)
7 oz (200 g) whole grain
   shortbread biscuits
½ cup (100 g) butter, melted
1 ⅓ cups (300 g) cream cheese
   (full fat)
1 cup + 2 tsp (250 g) crème fraîche
2 tbsp (25 g) sugar
•14.1 oz (400 g) ripe strawberries,
   washed and cut into small pieces

♥

ADDITIONALLY:
⅓ cup + 1 tbsp (100 ml) cream
A few visually appealing
   strawberries for decorating

1. Grind the biscuits finely and mix in a bowl with the melted butter. Then pour the mixture onto the bottom of the springform pan or pie pan and press down firmly. Place the pan in the refrigerator.

2. Meanwhile, mix the cream cheese and crème fraîche well in a bowl. Then add the sugar and mix everything together.

3. Fold in the strawberries carefully, and then take the pan out of the refrigerator. Evenly distribute the cream cheese mixture on top of the crust.

4. Keep the pie in the refrigerator overnight. The next day, before serving, garnish with whipped cream and strawberries.

Rhubarb Pie

It looks complicated, but in reality, it's super easy. Because of the lattice, this pie only reveals its secret upon the first bite, when the fantastically sweet and sour rhubarb-orange filling tickles the tongue.

FOR 1 PIE PAN (9 IN / 23 CM DIAMETER)

♥

FOR THE CRUST:
2 ½ cups + 1 tsp (315 g) flour
1 pinch salt
1 tsp sugar
¾ cup + 2 tsps (190 g) very cold butter, cut into pieces
½ cup + 1 tbsp (125 ml) ice cold water

♥

FOR THE FILLING:
26.5 oz (750 g) rhubarb, washed and diced
1 ½ cups (300 g) sugar
3 tbsp cornstarch
Juice and zest from one organic orange
1 egg yolk, lightly whisked
1 tbsp granulated brown sugar

♥

ADDITIONALLY:
Flour for the countertop

1. Mix the flour, salt, and sugar. Add the butter and mix everything rapidly until the mixture is crumbly.

2. Add the water and combine everything (again, quickly) into a dough. If it is too dry, add another tablespoon of water until it holds together.

3. Divide the dough into two equal pieces and lightly press until flat. Wrap in plastic wrap and refrigerate for at least ½ hour.

4. Next take ½ of the dough out of the refrigerator, roll out on a lightly floured countertop and lay out in the pan. Let the dough extend slightly over the edge of the pan.

5. For the filling, mix rhubarb, sugar, starch, orange juice and orange zest in a bowl, and then pour into the pie pan.

6. Preheat the oven to 430°F (220°C), using both top and bottom heat.

7. Roll the remaining dough out so that it is a little bit larger than the pan, and cut with a pizza cutter into 12 strips. Now lay this dough out like a grid on the pie (see p. 106). Tuck the edges under the pie crust and seal together.

8. Brush the pie with the whisked egg yolk and sprinkle with granulated brown sugar. Bake for approximately 1 hour in the oven. Allow to cool before serving.

Pear Tart Tatin

WITH CRÈME FRAÎCHE

Since I have made my peace with pears, and use them more often for baking now, the tart tatin version is also more commonly seen slipping out of my oven. Please repeat after me: "I made a TART TATAAHN OH POAAR" Sounds nice, right? You feel the little French girl coming out in you a little more. And it just feels great.

FOR 1 TART TATIN PAN
OR OVEN-SAFE PAN
(APPROX. 12 IN / 30 CM
DIAMETER)
3 small pears
A little bit of lemon juice
¾ cup (150 g) sugar
3 tbsp butter, cut into slices
1 roll puff pastry out of the
   refrigerated section (not frozen!)

♥

ADDITIONALLY:
1 cup (200 g) crème fraîche for
   serving

1. Preheat the oven to 390°F (200°C).

2. Peel the pears into quarters and remove the seeds. Immediately mix with the lemon juice and ¼ cup (50 g) of sugar in a bowl, and set aside.

3. Add the remaining sugar to a small, oven-safe pan or a special tart tatin pan, and caramelize by stirring on the stove over medium heat. Once the sugar is liquid, carefully place the pear quarters on top of the caramel, with the round sides facing down, or lay out in the form of a star. Add the butter to the pears and let everything simmer for about 5 minutes.

4. Cut a circle out of the puff pastry, a little bit bigger than the diameter of the pan. Now place the puff pastry on top of the pears, and using a knife, turn down the edges of the dough so that the pears are wrapped well. In the middle of the dough, cut a small cross, so that heat can escape. Then bake in the oven for ½ hour.

5. Finally, take the tart from the oven, let it sit for 5 minutes, and then gently remove from the pan. The best way to do this is to place a plate over the pan, and flip it over quickly, so that you do not have to have hot caramel sauce running over your fingers.

6. Voila, the tart can now be served with crème fraîche.

MY TIP

Cream or ice cream also tastes good with this tart.

Almond Tart

WITH CREAM CHEESE FROSTING, NECTARINES, AND BERRIES

What's especially nice about this tart: It is so colorful. And if you'd like, it can be even more colorful. Cherries, plums, apricots . . . Anything that you can find in your garden or farmer's market can adorn this tart.

FOR 1 RECTANGULAR
TART FORM (13 ¾ X 4 ½ IN /
35 X 11 CM,
PREFERABLY WITH A
REMOVABLE BOTTOM)

♥

FOR THE CRUST:
1 ⅔ cups (200 g) flour
¼ cup (25 g) ground almonds
⅔ cup (80 g) powdered sugar
1 pinch salt
½ cup + ½ tbsp (120 g) very cold
    butter, cut into pieces
1 egg

♥

FOR THE FILLING:
⅔ cup (150 g) cream cheese
½ cup (120 g) crème fraîche
4 tbsp powdered sugar
3 nectarines, washed and cut
    into slices
Berries as desired (or cherries,
plums, apricots, or others)

♥

ADDITIONALLY:
Flour for the countertop
Butter for the pan

1. For the dough, mix flour, almonds, powdered sugar, and salt. Add the butter and rub with your hands until crumbly.

2. Then add the egg, and combine everything quickly into a smooth dough. Shape it into a ball, wrap it in plastic wrap, and refrigerate for 1 hour.

3. Then remove the dough from the refrigerator and roll it out on the floured countertop until it is slightly larger than the tart pan. Place in the lightly buttered pan, press it in, and remove excess dough from the edges. Put the pan, as well as the dough, in the refrigerator for another ½ hour.

4. Preheat the oven to 375°C (190°C), using both top and bottom heat.

5. Poke the dough at the bottom of the pan several times with a fork and bake for 15–20 minutes in the oven. Then let cool completely.

6. In the meantime, mix cream cheese, crème fraîche, and powdered sugar into a creamy filling with a hand mixer, and refrigerate for 1 hour.

7. Then pour the filling onto the dough, distribute the nectarine slices and berries, and enjoy the tart immediately.

IN
Chocolate Heaven

Cocoa beans are probably my favorite beans. Here's to the Maya, who
cultivated them, and the sailors who brought this brown gold to Europe.
Because it can melt us in so many ways: fruit dipped in chocolate,
chocolate-infused cakes, tarts with chocolate, cookies. All of these very different
foods are connected to each other through chocolate. It is something that can
really bring people happiness, and I know, that with this ingredient, I've got
something for any situation in the pantry.

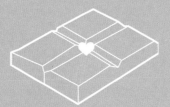

Chocolate Tart

WITH MERINGUE

In a way, this one is a wolf in sheep's clothing. You first glance at the meringues and see cotton-soft clouds, and don't discover the chocolatey secret until after the fork has dived into the chocolate sea—how heavenly!

FOR 1 TART PAN WITH A
REMOVABLE BOTTOM
(9 IN / 23 CM DIAMETER)

♥

FOR THE CRUST:
1 cup (125 g) flour
1 pinch salt
½ cup (40 g) unsweetened
  high-quality cocoa powder
½ cup (115 g) room temperature
  butter
⅓ cup (60 g) sugar
1 egg
3 tbsp cream

♥

FOR THE FILLING:
4 tbsp chocolate spread
6.3 oz (180 g) milk chocolate,
  finely chopped
⅓ cup (80 g) heavy cream

♥

FOR THE MERINGUE:
4 egg whites
1 cup + 2 tbsp (225 g) fine sugar

1. For the dough, mix flour, salt, and cocoa powder in a bowl. In another bowl, mix the butter and sugar until creamy, then add the egg. Alternate adding the flour mixture and cream, a little at a time, and combine everything into a smooth dough. Lightly press it flat and wrap in plastic wrap. Store in the refrigerator for at least 1 hour.

2. Preheat the oven to 345°F (175°C).

3. Roll out the dough and place it into the tart pan. Poke a fork into it multiple times, and bake for about 20 minutes in the oven. Let cool completely, and brush with the chocolate spread.

4. Melt the chocolate with heavy cream in a double boiler, and let cool for about 5 minutes. Then spread this mixture out on the bottom of the tart and set in the refrigerator for about 2 hours.

5. Just before serving, beat the egg whites with sugar until they are very stiff, and then spread onto the cake. Make sure that the entire chocolate surface is covered with egg white. Let brown under a hot broiler for about 5 minutes. Then serve and enjoy.

Brownies
WITH RED WINE GANACHE

This is another all-time favorite of my two men. For the little ones, there's a nonalcoholic version, but for the older ones, the brownies are best enriched with a good red wine in the ganache.

FOR A RECTANGULAR BAKING
PAN (9 X 13 IN / 23 X 33 CM)

♥

FOR THE CRUST:
1 cup + 3 tbsp (150 g) flour
1 tsp salt
2 tbsp unsweetened, good quality
   cocoa powder
10.6 oz (300 g) dark chocolate,
   coarsely chopped
1 cup (230 g) butter, cut into pieces
1 ¾ cups (350 g) white sugar
⅔ cup (125 g) granulated brown
   sugar
5 eggs
3.5 oz (100 g) walnuts, chopped

♥

FOR THE GANACHE
8.1 oz (230 g) dark chocolate,
   coarsely chopped
¾ cup (180 ml) cream
2 tbsp (30 g) butter
1 tbsp red wine

♥

ADDITIONALLY:
Butter for the pan

1. Preheat the oven to 345°F (175°C). Butter the baking pan and line the bottom with parchment paper.

2. For the dough, mix flour, salt, and cocoa powder in a bowl, then set aside.

3. Melt the chocolate with the butter in a double boiler. Then remove from heat, add the two types of sugar and let cool.

4. Add 3 eggs to the chocolate mixture and carefully mix under. Then add the remaining eggs and mix into a homogeneous mass. Under no circumstances should you should stir too much, or the brownies will be rock hard.

5. Sift the flour mixture over the chocolate and fold in. Do not mix. Fold in only until no more clumps of flour can be seen. Fold in the nuts briefly also. Then fill the pan evenly with dough.

6. Bake the brownies in the oven for ½ hour and allow to cool. They might be a bit soft, but that is a good thing. That is typical brownie consistency.

7. For the ganache, put the chocolate in a glass bowl. Bring the cream and butter to a boil in a small pot over medium heat, and then pour immediately over the chocolate. Let stand briefly, and then stir very gently, so that no air comes into the ganache. Mix in the red wine, and then spread on top of the brownies. Once the ganache is hard enough, cut the brownies to the desired size.

Chocolate Truffle Tart

WITH RASPBERRIES

This velvety-soft chocolate sin is the very definition of dessert. It is not baked, and glides so smoothly off the fork into your mouth. And I particularly love to top it with fresh fruit.

FOR 1 SMALL SPRINGFORM
PAN (6 IN / 16 CM DIAMETER)
8.8 oz (250 g) high-quality
    dark chocolate, chopped coarsely
1 cup + ½ tbsp (250 ml) cream
1 pinch cinnamon
Cocoa powder for sprinkling
8.8 oz (250 g) raspberries (or other
    berries)

1. Line the springform pan with parchment paper.

2. Melt the chocolate using a double boiler. Heat up the cream in a saucepan, and then remove from heat. Add chocolate and cinnamon to the cream. Stir until a smooth mass forms.

3. Pour the chocolate mixture into the springform pan and keep in a cool place for at least 4 hours.

4. Before serving, sprinkle with cocoa powder and garnish with fresh berries.

Cocoa Biscotti
WITH PISTACHIO

The pistachio tree is a deciduous tree that can grow up to 12 feet high and live up to 300 years. They're definitely determined. But the pistachio is, above all, a wonderful ingredient that makes these biscotti crunchy and gives them that little something extra.

MAKES APPROX. 48 PIECES

2 ½ cups (300 g) flour

1 tsp baking powder

3 tbsp (30 g) unsweetened high-quality cocoa powder

¾ cup (175 ml) vegetable oil

3 eggs

1 cup + 2 tbsp (225 g) sugar

2 ½ oz (70 g) shelled, unsalted pistachios

1. Mix the flour, baking powder, and cocoa powder, sift into a bowl and set aside.

2. In another bowl, mix eggs and oil, and then add the sugar. Add the flour mixture a little bit at a time, increasing the mixing speed gradually, until the dough is a homogeneous mass. Then fold in the pistachios.

3. Cover the dough with plastic wrap and refrigerate for at least 1 hour.

4. Preheat the oven to 345°F (175°C). Line a baking sheet with parchment paper.

5. Divide the dough into two pieces and form each into a 12-in (30 cm) long roll on the parchment paper. Apply light pressure with a rolling pin, so that they are 3 in (8-9 cm) wide. Bake for 25 minutes in the oven.

6. Then take the baking sheet out of the oven, and reduce the temperature to 300°F (150°C).

7. Allow the rolls to cool almost completely, and then carefully cut into approximately ½-in (1 ½ cm) thick slices. Then lay these out flat next to each other on the baking sheet and bake once again for 15 minutes.

MY TIP

If desired, pour melted chocolate over the biscotti.

White Chocolate Blondies
WITH WALNUTS

White brownies are fittingly called blondies. Here the blondes get together, meet crispy walnuts, and delight every fan of white chocolate.

FOR 2 SQUARE BAKING PANS
(8 X 8 IN / 20 X 20 CM
DIAMETER)

5 ¼ oz (150 g) white chocolate,
   roughly chopped
⅔ cup (150 g) butter
⅔ cup (150 g) sugar
2 eggs
1 pinch of salt
1 ⅔ cups (200 g) flour
2 handfuls of walnuts, chopped

♥

ADDITIONALLY:
Butter for the pan

1. Preheat oven to 356°F (180°C). Butter the pan and line with parchment paper.

2. Melt butter and chocolate in a double boiler. Let cool for a moment.

3. In the meantime, beat the eggs, salt, and sugar until foamy using a hand mixer. Then add in the chocolate mixture.

4. Sift the flour in and mix under well. Fold the walnuts in.

5. Fill the prepared pan with dough, and bake for about ½ hour. Let cool, and cut the blondies into squares.

Apple-Chocolate
CAKE

We love apples, and whenever our little, old, gnarly apple tree holds fresh fruits for us in autumn, we'll have apple pancakes, applesauce, apple crumble and all sorts of apple cakes. To introduce some apple-related diversity to our diet (and my oven) I created an apple-chocolate cake. I'm gonna lean myself reallllly far out of the window here and share this with the world: This is my new favorite apple recipe—AND favorite chocolate cake.

FOR 1 SPRINGFORM PAN
(8 IN / 20 CM DIAMETER)

3 small apples

A little bit of lemon juice

8.8 oz (250 g) dark chocolate, roughly chopped

¾ cup + 1 tbsp (160 ml) cream

3 eggs, separated

4 tbsp cornstarch

3 tbsp honey or maple syrup

3 tbsp ground hazelnuts (almonds, walnuts, or others)

1 tbsp brown sugar

♥

ADDITIONALLY:
Butter for the pan

1. Preheat the oven to 375°F (190°C). Line the springform pan with parchment paper and butter the rim.

2. Peel the apples, remove the seeds and the stems, dice, sprinkle with some lemon juice, and then put aside.

3. Place chopped chocolate in a bowl. Bring cream to a boil in a pot and pour over the chocolate immediately. Let it sit for a moment, and then stir until it becomes a sinfully creamy and chocolatey mass.

4. Slowly mix in the egg yolks. Only add the next egg yolk once the previous one has been completely stirred in. Mix in the cornstarch as well.

5. Beat the egg whites to stiff peaks and mix in the honey (or maple syrup) as well. Place a third of the egg-white mixture in with the chocolate dough and mix well. Then gently fold the rest of the egg-white mixture in.

6. Pour the dough into the pan, spread it around, and cover with the apples. Sprinkle with ground up hazelnuts (or any other nuts) and granulated brown sugar.

7. Bake the cake for 35–40 minutes. After this, the cake should be somewhat moist, like a brownie, so don't bake it for too long.

8. Let it cool down a little, and remove from the pan.

Red Velvet Cake

The red color in the cake was originally caused by the reaction between the cocoa powder and buttermilk. Nowadays, we enhance that effect with food coloring so we can conjure up a cake that looks like it came out of a fairy tale.

FOR 3 SPRINGFORM PANS
(8 IN / 20 CM DIAMETER)

♥

FOR THE DOUGH:
1 cup + 1 ½ tbsp (250 g) room
   temperature butter
3 ⅓ cups (660 g) sugar
6 eggs
2 tbsp (30 ml) red liquid food
   coloring
3 tbsp unsweetened high-grade
   cocoa powder
3 cups (375 g) flour
1 cup + 1 tbsp (250 ml) buttermilk
½ tsp salt
1 tsp baking soda
1 tbsp white wine vinegar

♥

FOR THE FROSTING:
3 tbsp + 1 tsp (50 g) room
   temperature butter
½ cup (100 g) room temperature
   cream cheese
1 ¼ cups (250 g) powdered sugar,
   plus a little extra

♥

ADDITIONALLY:
Butter and flour for the pans

1. Preheat the oven to 340°F (170°C). Butter and flour the springform pans. Line the bottoms with parchment paper.

2. Beat the butter and sugar using a mixer, until foamy. Slowly add the eggs.

3. Stir the food coloring together with the cocoa powder until it's creamy, and add to the dough as well.

4. Alternate between adding flour and buttermilk, and then add salt.

5. Dissolve the baking soda in vinegar and mix in with the dough as well. Now, evenly distribute the dough between the three pans, and let bake in the oven for about 25 minutes. Let cool, and then remove the cake layers from the pans.

6. For the frosting, mix butter and cream cheese until creamy. Add powdered sugar, and combine everything together into a spreadable mass. For that, you will have to stir a little longer, so don't give up, it'll get there! If after a lot of stirring the mixture is still too tough, simply add a little milk. If it seems too liquidy, add more powdered sugar.

7. Now spread frosting on the first layer of cake, and place the second layer of cake on top, then frost again. Once all three layers are stacked, spread the frosting around the sides and the top as well. Keep refrigerated until consumption.

MY TIP

Those who don't own 3 springform pans can bake the layers one after another in one pan.

Chocolate Truffles

Cute little balls of chocolate are always smiling at me when I pass a chic patisserie in my hometown. But even still, it's really not too difficult to roll them up yourself. And the beautiful part is: you can flavor them however you'd like. Vanilla, espresso, chili, hazelnut liquor, cinnamon . . . In this case, I chose cardamom. Those who don't like cardamom can simply leave it out, or replace it with something more to their liking.

MAKES APPROX. 30 TRUFFLES

8 ounces (225 g) dark chocolate

1 cup (250 ml) cream

1 pinch ground cardamom

3 tbsp + 2 ½ tsp (55 g) butter

Cocoa powder, for tossing

1. Chop up the chocolate very finely.

2. Bring the cream to a boil, together with the cardamom, and pour over the chocolate. Stir well, until a smooth chocolate cream has formed. Slowly stir in the butter.

3. Let the chocolate mixture cool in the refrigerator for 15 minutes. Afterward, use a teaspoon to carve out little balls, and keep them cold for 1 hour.

4. Lastly, toss the chocolate truffles in cocoa powder.

MY TIP

These delicious balls of chocolate are easily packaged and make a great gift for family or friends.

Chocolate Shortbread Cookies

WITH VANILLA SALT

These tasty chocolate biscuits with delicate, contrasting vanilla salt say "Hello," even when the word is not stamped on them. But just in case you forget to gobble them all down, I wrote it on the cookies once more, just to be on the safe side.

MAKES 8 SHORTBREAD
COOKIES

½ cup (60 g) powdered sugar

5 tbsp (70 g) room temperature
butter

4 ½ tbsp (60 g) vegetable oil

1 cup (125 g) flour

3 tbsp unsweetened, high-quality
cocoa powder

1 pinch of salt

A little bit of vanilla salt for
sprinkling

1. Place sugar, butter, and oil in a bowl and mix well.

2. Briefly mix the flour, cocoa powder, and salt before sifting into the butter mixture. Using your hands, knead into an even dough, and wrap up in plastic wrap. Refrigerate for about ½ hour.

3. In the meantime, preheat the oven to 320°F (160°C). Line a baking sheet with parchment paper.

4. Roll out the dough into a 1-cm-thick circle, sprinkle with a little vanilla salt, poke repeatedly using a fork, and bake for about ½ hour.

5. Take the shortbread out of the oven and cut into 8 pieces. Allow it to cool and enjoy.

MY TIP

Several spice retailers sell vanilla salt, but you can also easily prepare it yourself. Remove the pulp from 4 vanilla pods, and place it on top of 1 cup of sea salt. Now rub the vanilla pulp into the salt using a pestle or a spoon, and store well sealed.

Chocolate-Covered Strawberries

WITH A TWIST

Who said that strawberries have to be covered in chocolate individually?
With that in mind, we'll now take 8 or 10 strawberries at once and do this a little bit differently.
At least 8 to 10 times as tasty!

MAKES 10 ½ OZ (300 G)
CHOCOLATE-COVERED
STRAWBERRIES
5 ⅓ ounces (150 g) milk chocolate
5 ⅓ ounces (150 g) dark chocolate
8 large strawberries

1. Line a small loaf pan with a cut-out piece of freezer bag.

2. Chop up both types of chocolate and melt them together in a double boiler.

3. Spread a thin layer of chocolate over the bottom of the pan.

4. Wash the strawberries, remove the leaves, and cut off the tops in such a way that they can stand upside down.

5. Place the fruit on top of the chocolate in the pan and pour the rest of the chocolate over the strawberries. Let sit (possibly in the refrigerator) until hard. Then take the chocolate-covered strawberries out of the pan.

MY TIP

Serve the chocolate-covered strawberries ice cold in the summer.

Chocolate Coconut

SCONES

Delicious scones are the perfect breakfast for a Sunday morning. Aside from that, they're also a beautiful adornment on any breakfast or brunch table. These convenient little treats—in this case with coconut flavor—are also excellent for bringing on picnics.

MAKES 8 SCONES

2 ⅓ cups + ½ tbsp (300 g) flour

2 tbsp brown sugar

1 tbsp baking powder

1 pinch of salt

½ cup (115 g) cold butter cut into pieces

1 handful of chocolate pieces (chopped chocolate or chocolate chips)

½ cup (120 ml) coconut milk

2 eggs

♥

ADDITIONALLY:

Flour for kneading

2 tbsp coconut milk

3 tbsp brown sugar

1. Preheat oven to 390°F (200°C).

2. Mix flour, sugar, baking powder and salt. Add butter and crumble everything together with your hands. Now add in chocolate chips.

3. Whisk together coconut milk and eggs, and add to the flour mix. With well-floured hands knead into an even dough. If the dough is too sticky, add more flour.

4. Spread the dough into an approx. 1 ½-inch (4 cm) thick circle on a baking tray lined with parchment paper and divide into eight pieces using a sharp knife. Baste with coconut milk and sprinkle with sugar. (Do not pull the eight pieces apart, but instead put the entire piece of dough into the oven just as it is.)

5. Bake the scones for 15–20 minutes, and enjoy while they are still warm.

MY TIP

True Brits would probably top these with clotted cream. You can also eat them with marmalade, however, or crème fraîche, lightly beaten cream, butter, maple syrup . . . Or purely natural is also an excellent alternative.

Blueberry Torte

WITH WHITE CHOCOLATE FROSTING

You're looking for a heavenly little cake for a Sunday afternoon in the garden? Well, here it is. Cloaked with sweet frosting on the outside, and with delicious blueberries as a light, refreshing contrast. Set up some lawn chairs and a table outside, cover the table with a tablecloth, and enjoy.

FOR 2 SPRINGFORM PANS
(8 IN / 20 CM DIAMETER)

♥

FOR THE DOUGH:
3 ⅔ cups + 3 tbsp (450 g) flour
3 ½ tsp baking powder
1 pinch of salt
1 cup + 5 tsp (250 g) room
   temperature butter
2 ¼ cups (450 g) sugar
Scraped out pulp of 1 vanilla pod
4 eggs
1 cup + 1 tbsp (250 ml) milk
14 oz (400 g) blueberries

♥

FOR THE FROSTING:
6 oz (170 g) high-quality white
   chocolate, roughly chopped
¼ cup (60 ml) cream
1 cup (230 g) room temperature
   butter
1 cup + 2 tsp (125 g) powdered sugar

♥

ADDITIONALLY:
Butter and flour for the pans
2 tbsp blueberry marmalade
   for decoration

1. Preheat oven to 355°F (180°C). Butter and flour the pans.

2. For the dough, sift flour, baking powder, and salt into a bowl, and set aside.

3. Stir butter, sugar, and vanilla pulp with a hand mixer until creamy. Add the eggs in one by one.

4. Now alternate between kneading the flour mixture and the milk into the dough.

5. Toss 3 tbsp of blueberries in flour (so that the berries don't sink to the bottom during baking), and fold them carefully into the dough.

6. Now evenly distribute the dough between the two pans and bake for 30–40 minutes in the oven. Let cool, and then remove from the pans.

7. For the frosting, melt the white chocolate with the cream in a double boiler. Let cool (important!), and then add butter and powdered sugar. Beat using a hand mixer, until the mixture is spreadable.

8. Now spread the frosting thinly on top of the first layer of cake, spread blueberry marmalade over that, and place the second layer of cake on top. Spread the rest of the frosting on top of and on the sides of the cake, and garnish with blueberries.

Chocolate Chestnut

CAKE

Sweet chestnuts are not just what you can buy at Christmas markets to warm your frozen limbs. They also taste wonderful with chocolate, and particularly as an ingredient of this cake.

FOR 1 SPRINGFORM PAN
(9.5 IN / 24 CM DIAMETER)
10.5 oz (300 g) dark chocolate
15.3 oz (435 g) sweet chestnut
    puree (can)
½ cup + 1 tsp (150 g) crème fraîche
3 ½ tbsp (50 g) room temperature
    butter
4 egg whites
6 ½ tbsp (80 g) sugar
6 tbsp flour

♥

ADDITIONALLY:
Butter for the pan

1. Preheat oven to 300°F (150°C). Butter the pan and line it with parchment paper.

2. Roughly chop the chocolate, melt it in a double boiler, and put aside.

3. Pour the chestnut puree into a bowl and mix with crème fraîche and butter.

4. Beat egg whites until stiff, and add sugar little by little.

5. Stir the flour into the chocolate, and then thoroughly combine that mixture with the chestnut cream.

6. Stir ⅓ of the beaten egg whites in with the chocolate dough, and carefully fold in the rest.

7. Fill the pan with dough, and then knock it several times onto the countertop so that the dough spreads out evenly.

8. Bake the cake in the oven for about 50 minutes. Then let it cool off.

MY TIP

If desired, you can dust the cake with cocoa powder and serve along with vanilla ice cream.

MINT
Ice Box Cake

A real childhood classic that I've matured a bit with a peppermint twist. That's what I thought at least, until the kids ended up liking it just as much as the grown-ups did and the entire cake was gone in moments.

FOR 1 VERY SMALL
CHILDREN'S LOAF PAN
(double the amounts when
using a regular-sized loaf pan)

3 oz (75 g) dark chocolate,
  roughly chopped
7 oz (200 g) milk chocolate,
  roughly chopped
14 pieces of chocolate with
  mint filling (i.e., Andes)
2.6 oz (75 g) Copha (solidified
  coconut fat)
⅓ cup + 2 tbsp (100 ml) cream
2 tsp (8 g) vanilla sugar
4.4 oz (125 g) butter cookies

1. Let the chocolate, Copha and cream slowly melt in a pot on medium heat. Add vanilla sugar and let the whole mass cool down.

2. Line the loaf pan with plastic wrap or aluminum foil. Place a little bit of the chocolate mass at the bottom of the pan, and then alternate between layering on cookies and chocolate. Finish with a layer of chocolate.

3. Into the fridge with that nugget of culinary gold! Let the the icebox cake cool and harden for about 6 hours.

4. Remove from the pan by flipping the pan over, take the pan liner off the cake, cut yourself off a piece, and enjoy.

DOUBLE CHOCOLATE
Cocoa Cake

As soon as it was out of the oven, it was gone. How did that happen? One free afternoon, with two schoolmates at our house, made for three hungry mouths to feed. To this day, the boys are still asking: "Did your mom bake again?"

FOR 1 MEDIUM-SIZED
BUNDT PAN

♥

FOR THE DOUGH:
1 ¾ cups + 2 tbsp (230 g) flour
5 tbsp unsweetened high-grade
   cocoa powder
1 tbsp baking powder
1 pinch of salt
4 eggs
1 cup + 2 tbsp (220 g) sugar
1 cup (240 ml) milk
½ cup (125 g) butter, cut into
   pieces

♥

FOR THE GLAZE:
¼ cup (60 ml) milk
7 oz (200 g) milk chocolate,
   chopped

♥

ADDITIONALLY:
Butter and flour for the pan
3.5 oz (100 g) milk chocolate for
   garnishing

1. Preheat oven to 355°F (180°C) plastic wrap or aluminum foil. Butter and flour the pan.

2. For the dough, mix flour, cocoa powder, baking powder, and salt, sift into a bowl, and put aside.

3. Mix eggs and sugar using a hand mixer until the mass is light and creamy. Then combine thoroughly with the flour mixture.

4. Let milk and butter simmer over low heat, until the butter is melted. Add this mixture to the dough, and stir until a homogeneous mixture results.

5. Fill the prepared pan with dough and bake for 20–25 minutes. (Do the toothpick test!) Remove from the pan and let cool.

6. For the glaze, bring the milk to a boil in a small pot, immediately take off the stove, and pour over the chopped chocolate. Let the mixture sit for a moment, stir once and carefully glaze the cake with it.

7. Melt the remaining chocolate in a double boiler and immediately pour onto a piece of parchment paper. Quickly and carefully roll the parchment paper up and allow the chocolate to stiffen in the refrigerator. Once you unroll the paper, you'll find beautiful, wavy chocolate flakes. Garnish the bundt cake with these.

INDEX

For Henri, the sweetest thing in my life

Copyright © 2015 by Virginia Horstmann

Skyhorse Publishing books may be purchased in bulk at special discounts for sales promotion, corporate gifts, fund-raising, or educational purposes. Special editions can also be created to specifications. For details, contact the Special Sales Department, Skyhorse Publishing, 307 West 36th Street, 11th Floor, New York, NY 10018 or info@skyhorsepublishing.com.

Skyhorse® and Skyhorse Publishing® are registered trademarks of Skyhorse Publishing, Inc.®, a Delaware corporation.

Visit our website at www.skyhorsepublishing.com.

10 9 8 7 6 5 4 3 2 1

Library of Congress Cataloging-in-Publication Data is available on file.

Cover design by Tanja Kapahnke
Cover photo credit: Virginia Horstmann (excluding the top right photo on front cover and back cover photo)
Photos: Virginia Horstmann, except photos from the front-end and back-end pages, photos on pg 1, pg 2, pg 8 (left center), pg 42 (top center), pg 80 (top right, bottom center), pg 106 (top right), and pg 142 (top right)
Illustrations: Julia Marquardt • Editing (German edition): Christin Geweke • Image editing: Lisa Frischemeier

Print ISBN: 978-1-63220-671-8
Ebook ISBN: 978-1-63220-905-4

Printed in China